PENGUIN BOOKS

NEW WORLD UTOPIAS

Paul Kagan was born in Chicago in 1943. In 1965 he received his degree in history from the University of California at Berkeley. Since then, his career has included work as a television news writer, a photographer, and a magazine art director. While writing *New World Utopias* he collected valuable historical materials and went on to found the Utopian Studies Center at the California Historical Society Library. He currently lives in San Francisco.

NEW WORLD

UTOPIAS

A PHOTOGRAPHIC HISTORY OF THE SEARCH FOR COMMUNITY

by Paul Kagan

PENGUIN BOOKS

Penguin Books Inc, 72 Fifth Avenue,
New York, New York 10011, U.S.A.
Penguin Books Inc, 7110 Ambassador Road,
Baltimore, Maryland 21207, U.S.A.
Penguin Books Ltd, Harmondsworth,
Middlesex, England
Penguin Books Australia Ltd, Ringwood,
Victoria, Australia
Penguin Books Canada Limited, 41 Steelcase Road West,
Markham, Ontario, Canada L3R 1B4
Penguin Books (N.Z.) Ltd, 182–190 Wairau Road,
Auckland 10, New Zealand

First published 1975

Copyright © Paul Kagan, 1975

Library of Congress Catalog Card Number: 74-78929

Printed in the United States of America

Designed by A. Christopher Simon

To John Pentland

Preface

In 1967 I became interested in the newly emerging communes in the western United States. At the same time I wondered about the past. What had people tried communally before? What had they found out, and what had they left? What had become of the earlier communes and their inhabitants?

Two events spurred my interest on. A slide lecture about the Shakers in early nineteenth-century America made me wonder what had happened to the vitality of these communes. Shaker work left impressive visible traces that can be seen today in Shaker buildings. I wondered what would have allowed these communes to endure.

Then I photographed the activities at a present-day New Mexico commune and experienced a little of the life there. It seemed to me that problems in communal living—such as how to reconcile personal with group interests—were echoed both in individuals and in our larger national community.

To find out more about communal experiences, I began to look into the history of communes in California. I learned that there were scores of communes in California long before 1970. Since I wanted to photograph the remains of communal endeavor, there had to be visible evidence of the commune's past if I was to include it in my study.

The span of time is approximately the century from 1870 to 1970. The groups vary from the religious to the occult to the political, and I found their ruins in the deserts and mountains and on the seashore in northern and southern California. As I studied these groups, I began to interview survivors and to collect photographs and documents that were made at the time the communes existed. There was more knowledge and a much richer life than I had suspected. I was continually surprised by the fragments of understanding and the strange energies that I encountered.

Much of the life, and much of the story, is in the photographs. The photographs that I made represent my feelings about the communal remains, and the historical photographs show a little of the daily life of the groups. The accompanying text tells the communal history and, hopefully, raises some pertinent questions.

P. K.
San Francisco
June, 1974

7

Acknowledgments

A five-year research and field project like this depends on the help of a great many people. Professor Robert V. Hine, at the University of California, Riverside, gave me the most gracious and unselfish help possible, his encouragement, criticism, and continuing interest, as well as access to his personal files for his thesis and book, *California's Utopian Colonies* (San Marino, Calif.: Huntington Library, 1953). While I drew much valuable information from them, any mistakes are my own.

Mariam Kagan contributed greatly to the writing and editing of early drafts of Chapters 2 through 8. Frederic Anderson, editor of the Mark Twain Papers at the University of California, Berkeley, carefully edited most of the early manuscript, as did Ruth Grodzins, of Midway Editorial Research in Chicago. I am grateful to them.

J. S. Holliday, executive director of the California Historical Society, added his striking vision and support during part of the research; he was instrumental in arranging an archive in the library of the California Historical Society for historical materials from California communes that I have collected and stored there. Paul Johnson, who was then director of publications, helped a great deal; many of the Llano del Rio picture captions are his. Peter Evans and Lynn Donovan, of the California Historical Society Library, have also helped greatly and given freely of their time.

Part of the early research was assisted with funds from the National Institute of Mental Health, which came with the help of Bennett Berger at the University of California.

I am greatly indebted to the liberal kindness of James D. Hart, William M. Roberts, and Irene Moran, of the Bancroft Library. Other libraries that were of specific use are credited in the photograph captions. Rob Haeseler, of the San Francisco *Chronicle* city desk, went out of his way to help, particularly with the photographs of Holy City.

Others who helped in the overall preparation of the book were Richard Rose, my agent, and Don Burns, my editor at Penguin Books. Don recognized the book as a photo-history and spent long and tireless hours with me selecting photographs from the thousands I had made and collected, writing captions, and solving editorial difficulties. He was a warm and sympathetic editor and a friend in the midst of the gruesome hassles of putting the book together.

The Fountaingrove chapter merits specific thanks to Gaye LeBaron, who let me draw freely from her collection of original prints and also her excellent manuscript. Thanks are due, too, to the Columbia University Libraries and Tim Huston, of the Santa Rosa Public Library.

I am indebted to Ernest Marchand, of San Diego, for his criticisms of my Icaria Speranza chapter and his generous contribution of original photographs of

Icaria and a letter, in his possession, from that colony.

The people who helped with the chapter on the Theosophist communes were generous in their cooperation, but their approval is in no way implied. They include Professor Emmett Greenwalt, of California State University, Los Angeles; Judith Tyberg, of the East-West Cultural Center, Los Angeles; Iverson L. Harris, of San Diego; the late James A. Long, of Corona del Mar; Jack Rainey, of Los Angeles; Rosalind Rajagopal, Beatrice Wood, and Franklin Lacey, of Ojai; Betty Warrington, of Ojai; Harold Forgostein, of Halcyon; Grady Austin, of San Francisco; and Dorothy Varian, of Cupertino.

Much of the material on Llano del Rio comes from the Walter Millsap papers that I have stored in the California Historical Society Library; many of the photographs are by him. Some of the others were certainly taken by the colony photographer, Meyer Elkins; I thank his son Nathan and grandson Phillip for their courtesy. Jean Nourse and Bernie Stevens allowed me to use their extensive Llano papers. Mellie Calvert and Sarah Shuldiner were of help in my Llano research. Abraham Hoffman, of the University of Oklahoma, gave me a few good leads. Robert Weinstein, of Anderson, Ritchie & Simon, was encouraging and interested in my work. Dolores Hayden let me read portions of her unpublished manuscript. The extracts from Aldous Huxley's *Tomorrow and Tomorrow and Tomorrow* are reprinted by permission of Harper & Row, Publishers, Inc.

H. J. Smith allowed me to use pertinent Pisgah Grande materials in his possession. John Bartleman retold his experiences at old Pisgah to me. Edwin H. Carpenter, of the Huntington Library, furnished me with important Pisgah information, as did Ed Earl Repp.

Richard Baker, chief priest at the California Zen Center, was kind enough to read and criticize the Zen Center chapter. Katharine Thanas, Peter Schneider, Yvonne Rand, and Lucy Bennett also helped in different ways on that chapter. The extracts from *Wind Bell* are reprinted by permission of Harold Anderson, president of the Zen Center.

Special thanks to Professor Jacob Needleman, of San Francisco State University, for his help and encouragement.

Thanks also to Ralph Kagan, Marilyn Ziebarth, Muldoon Elder, Paul Reynard, Laura deWitt James, Sue Henderson, Ann Curtis, Roger Lipsey, Bruce Hamilton, Kenneth LaMott, David and Nancy Langmuir, Art Wadsworth, Mindy Scott, Molly Runkle, Albert and Roberta Wohlstetter, Dianne A. Smith, Leon and Esther Kagan, Beresford Parlett, David Smith, and Shigeyoshi Murao for their miscellaneous help.

Portions of this work have appeared in different form in the following publications: *California Historical Quarterly*, Vol. LI, No. 2 (Summer, 1972), and Vol. LII, No. 1 (Spring, 1973); *Maitreya I*, edited by Samuel Bercholz and Michael Fagan (Berkeley, Calif.: Shambala Publications, Inc., 1970); and *Religion for a New Generation*, edited by Jacob Needleman, A. K. Bierman, and James A. Gould (New York: The Macmillan Company, 1973).

Contents

Wagon trains like this one carried colonists to the West. Whole communes, such as the Bethel Rappites in Missouri, moved to the "New Eden." (Courtesy of the Association of American Railroads)

The Bethel commune in Missouri was a deeply religious group that descended indirectly from Harmony in Indiana. The colonists' strict rules did not prevent them from distilling Golden Rule whiskey. (From William Alfred Hinds, *American Communities & Co-operative Colonies* [2nd ed. rev., 1908; New York: Corinth Books, 1961])

CHAPTER 1

Utopia in the Nineteenth Century

In May of 1855, thirty-four covered prairie schooners were met on the Oregon Trail by a band of Sioux warriors avid to preserve their homeland. The sight at the head of the wagon train of a lead-lined casket bearing the body of a young man pickled in Golden Rule whiskey allayed the Indians' hostile intentions. It was not only the preserved body of Willie Keil that impressed the Sioux, but also the sight and sound of some 250 German Rappist colonists playing flutes, zithers, guitars, and drums and singing Martin Luther's "Eine feste Burg ist unser Gott." The Sioux could only declare it "strong medicine" and pass on their way.

These were the Bethel colonists, who had lived communally in Missouri and were following the westward course of empire to the Pacific coast. One of the community's popular contributions to Missouri society was the whiskey it made. Some of this alcohol was used to preserve the leader's son, Willie Keil, who in happier days had intended to lead the wagon train alive but who had died the day before departure.

The colonists were Rappites, and many of their practices were similar to those used in today's communes and throughout utopian history. They had come to America in 1805 and first settled at Harmony in Indiana, which was later sold to Robert Owen for his more political New Harmony. The Rappites later moved to Economy, on the East Coast. Rappite practices were in definite reaction to their times. They refused the use of stocks and pillories, and they generally imposed few sanctions. If a member failed to work for the good of the community, he could either leave voluntarily or be thrown out, rather than be physically punished. In spite of this lack of severe discipline, Harmony, like most utopias of the nineteenth century, was neat, orderly, and industrious, in contrast to a growing disorder in the surrounding towns and cities. These colonies were so oriented toward industry that Harmony was the first community to use steam power for manufacture.

The Rappites were ideologically influenced by an unlikely combination of Paracelsus, Plato, Jakob Böhme, and Alessandro di Cagliostro. The treatise of Harmony said, "Those who choose such a life . . . are conscious of their imperfections and dissatisfied with themselves." Those who joined then, as now, wished to achieve a synthesis of action and idea in the context of practical communal life.

By the early part of the nineteenth century in America there existed communities of transcendentalists, Fourierists, Perfectionists, Impressionists, Harmonists, Separatists, Millenarists, and Shakers, to name only a few. "Not a reading man but has a draft of a new community in his waistcoat pocket," wrote Ralph Waldo Emerson to Thomas Carlyle. "One man renounces the use of animal food; and another of coin;

13

Robert Owen's utopian socialist New Harmony community in Indiana settled on the same grounds occupied earlier by the religious Rappites. The change from "Harmony" to "New Harmony" and the attendant change of philosophy and people are typical of the movement of life through American communes.

"THE 'PROMISCUOUS,' 'BACK' OR 'QUICK' DANCE. From a contemporary engraving by A. Boyd Houghton. A spontaneous Shaker dance surviving from 1788, before organised and pattern dances were introduced. It was often revived, especially for children." Although Shaker practices, such as their dances and their strict celibacy, were criticized, Shaker communes led longer and more vital lives than many other American communes. (From William Alfred Hines, *American Communities & Co-operative Colonies*)

and another of domestic hired service; and another of the State." In this mélange of utopian life-styles the liberal, intellectual attractions of Emersonian transcendentalism are obvious. Emerson revived solar symbolism in a new way as he adopted ideas from the Orient. He spoke of the need "to guide our steps to the East again, where the dawn is." Emerson's commitment to traditional ideas is evident in his quoting Socrates's version of a much older idea, "The laws below are the sisters of the laws above."

In practical terms, at Brook Farm (a transcendentalist community founded in Massachusetts in 1841) this meant involving oneself in a new way with one's daily work. Although the bright clothes and light free walk of the transcendentalists were in striking contrast to the severity that surrounded their community, a rigorous work schedule prevailed, for which few of Emerson's intelligentsia were ready. The work provided a context for the sense of the present moment. It demanded the full participation of all members, including children. Brook Farm introduced kindergartens and anticipated John Dewey's dictum to "learn by experience" by emphasizing the study of nature through direct observation.

It was a transcendental ideal that man could master both his habits and his senses through the exertion of will by taking great nature as one's teacher. Emerson looked for a direct experience of God, as had Jonathan Edwards, but without a theological creed or an acknowledgment of original sin. Emerson's espousal of man's divinity revealed through nature opened the way for the introduction of Theosophical ideas later in the 1800's and for Theosophical experiments like Point Loma and Happy Valley in California a century later.

Although Emerson's influence on American utopian thinkers was great, Brook Farm itself was short-lived and, in practice, was corrupted by indolence. After a few years transcendentalism lost hold on the community, and a group of Fourierist socialists took over. Even Emerson himself soon lost interest in Brook Farm.

A few years later, the Oneida community was founded in New York, lasting from 1848 until 1881. It was remarkable in its time for combining the communism of economics with the communism of sex. Oneida also instituted a practice of "mutual criticism," aimed at self-examination as a safeguard against the authoritarian impulses of any hierarchy. A similar practice, in the form of a weekly "psychology" meeting, was held at Llano del Rio, and even today there are evening discussions in some of today's communes

The Amana commune led a rich and productive life in the Midwest. "Amana freezers" are household words today. (From William Alfred Hines, *American Communities & Co-operative Colonies*)

that are directly related to the Oneida mutual-criticism sessions.

John Humphrey Noyes, Oneida's leader and the author of *History of American Socialisms,* held that the American Indians were more Christian than their conquerors, a viewpoint shared by the Quakers and probably by many groups today. No American communal group ever seems to have had trouble with the Indians. In fact, there is a utopian tradition of learning from native Americans.

In the socioeconomic (nonreligious) communes of the nineteenth century Robert Owen and Charles Fourier were the two most important figures. Owen was born in 1771 and Fourier in 1772, and there is further synchronization in the appearance of their similar ideas at the same time, although in different places. At the time Owen acquired Harmony from the Rappites for his Indiana commune, he failed to recognize the naive nature of his utopian scheme. Like Fourier, he dealt only with the outside condition of man, convinced that if the social and economic influences improved, man would change. Owen tried experiments that dealt with the problems inherent in the traditional social and economic structure—but he quickly lost New Harmony to land speculators somewhat less naive than he.

Although it is evident that the religious communes generally outlived the socioeconomic ones in American history, the Fourierist phalanxes—as their settlements were called—were a strong and enduring force in America and, in fact, blended at times with American trade and commerce so much that the identities of the communities were destroyed. The Fourierist experiments began on the East Coast in 1843, but land was soon acquired for a phalanx in Texas. Fourierists also acquired the former Mormon temple and lands in Nauvoo, Illinois, and still another phalanx was organized in a former Shaker village. Icaria Speranza was a Fourierist offshoot.

The building of new colonies on land once occupied by earlier ones was coincidence or the result of efforts made by members of the original commune. More important was the migration of members of one community to another. Rappites became Shakers, and transcendentalists became Owenites. Some of these people probably moved because they could not have gotten along in any society, ideal or otherwise. Others were neither dilettantes nor misfits but men who were vaguely in search of something they could not identify and who were probably unaware of the forces that drew them from one commune to the next. There are parallels to this situation in the history of California's communes and in communal life today.

Most nineteenth-century communes, religious and socioeconomic, worked toward prison reform, an end to capital punishment, a solution to racial problems,

An oil painting (ca. 1844) by Josiah Wolcott of Brook Farm with its various buildings. Ralph Waldo Emerson and Louisa May Alcott were only two of the illustrious names that graced Brook Farm in the mid-1800's. (Courtesy of the Massachusetts Historical Society)

The Oneida community family, ca. 1860. John Humphrey Noyes, the leader of the commune, stands in the right foreground with his arms crossed. Oneida's remarkable philosophy included sexual experiments unusual for their time and selective-breeding experiments. (Photograph copyright © 1970 by Constance Noyes Robertson. From *Oneida Community: An Autobiography, 1851–1876*, edited by Constance Noyes Robertson [Syracuse, N.Y.: Syracuse University Press, 1970]. Photo reproduced by permission of the publisher.)

LOOKING BACKWARD

2000 — 1887

BY

EDWARD BELLAMY

Author of "*Miss Ludington's Sister*"; "*Dr. Heidenhoff's Process*";
"*A Nantucket Idyl*," &c., &c.

BOSTON
TICKNOR AND COMPANY
211 Tremont Street,
1888

Edward Bellamy's *Looking Backward* prompted the Bellamy clubs and a strange cooperation among seemingly diverse utopian thinkers in the late 1800's. Among these were labor leaders like Burnette G. Haskell, of the Kaweah Co-operative Commonwealth, mystics like Thomas Lake Harris, of Fountaingrove, and prominent Theosophists as well.

Social unrest and suffrage movements gave rise to groups like Llano del Rio and Kaweah in California's communal history. This is in Los Angeles around 1910. (Collection of Paul Kagan)

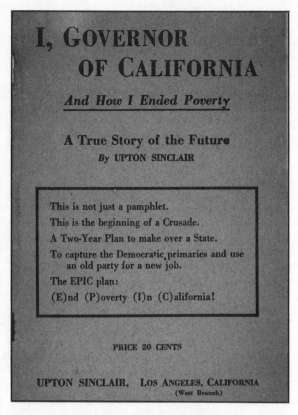

I, GOVERNOR OF CALIFORNIA

And How I Ended Poverty

A True Story of the Future
By UPTON SINCLAIR

> This is not just a pamphlet.
> This is the beginning of a Crusade.
> A Two-Year Plan to make over a State.
> To capture the Democratic primaries and use an old party for a new job.
> The EPIC plan:
> (E)nd (P)overty (I)n (C)alifornia!

PRICE 20 CENTS

UPTON SINCLAIR, LOS ANGELES, CALIFORNIA
(West Branch)

When Upton Sinclair ran for governor of California in 1934—and nearly won—he had the backing of both Theosophists and labor groups. Sinclair's sophisticated utopian political views were influenced by his alliance with social-reform causes and by the then-current Great Depression. (Collection of Paul Kagan)

female suffrage and other rights for women, a better agrarian and urban balance, and regulation of economic interests. These reformist causes represented only the external purposes of community life, however.

The period from 1888 to 1900 was a time of great proliferation of utopian visions. Edward Bellamy wrote *Looking Backward* in 1888, at a time of great unrest following the Civil War. Open cattle lands were being increasingly fenced and homesteaded for farming, and range wars ensued. Trains crossed the country; the frontier was rapidly closing. This, and more, contributed to the growth pains of a country originally "conceived in liberty" but now faced with the tasks of evaluating the meaning of democracy.

Bellamy's ideas had a direct influence on California communal history. His values were simple and honest: Man should strive toward perfection; the morals of

the social body should correspond to the morals of the individual; economic and social equality could do away with artificiality and repression. The power of his ideas led to the formation of a large number of Nationalist clubs, many in California, which did take part in bringing about some railway reforms. Bellamy's idea of nationalizing telephone and telegraph facilities under the U.S. Post Office Department was popular, although regrettably not accepted. Bellamy believed that *all* communication services should be nationalized, since he was wary of the influence of trusts and cartels on the communications media they owned. Of course, nationalization of the media would threaten the country's tradition of a free press, but Bellamy apparently believed in the possibility of an incorruptible government.

The utopian visions of the late nineteenth century were influenced by the fact that many of the earlier communal experiments had prospered economically. Finances were unbalanced at the time, and questions of money and labor were thrust into the public eye as part of a new examination of the meaning and sense of life. It was at this time that some of the early

Thomas More's *Utopia* was a sixteenth-century vision of an ideal community. Curiously, "utopia" means "nowhere."

California communal experiments began; among them were Kaweah, Fountaingrove, Point Loma, and Icaria Speranza.

Most utopian proposals of this period provided for communal housing, one universal tax, goods exchanged for services rather than money, circular cities (not unlike the geodesic domes and the radiating arrangement of the living structures of some of today's communes), simple clothing, no formal religion (reflected in the "nonsectarian" character of Theosophy and the "Christian anarchy" of Kaweah), compulsory cremation after death, and vegetarianism. One communal manual of the 1890's warned of the hazards of cooking with the dangerous metal aluminum—a belief still held by many interested in natural foods.

The communal tendencies of the nineteenth century were perhaps best summarized by John Humphrey Noyes, of Oneida: "The Revivalists had for their great idea the regeneration of the soul. The great idea of the Socialists was the regeneration of society, which is the soul's environment. These ideas belong together, and are the complements of each other."[1]

It is out of this soil and from this heritage that California's communal experiments grew. Today, members of communes are experiencing the same failures and accomplishments as their communal forefathers. If something more is known about the history of California's communes, would it lend a broader perspective to the problems of communal living today? It would seem that some lessons are learned only by experiencing them in the context of communal life, but that those interested in what a community means might profit from the study of past communal experiences.

In the following chapters a representative spectrum of historical California communes is presented. In conclusion there is an attempt to understand the questions posed by California's utopian history.

Thomas Lake Harris, the founder of Fountaingrove, was once described by William James as "America's best-known mystic." (Courtesy of the Columbia University Libraries)

CHAPTER 2

Fountaingrove

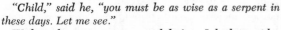

"Child," said he, "you must be as wise as a serpent in these days. Let me see."

With a dramatic gesture, and before I had any idea what he was about to do, he placed his hand on my solar plexus and gave a most unearthly grunt.

In this way a young lady from Boston was received by Thomas Lake Harris at Fountaingrove. Her story was published in the San Francisco *Chronicle* of December 13, 1891, under the headlines "HYPNOTIC HARRIS. Miss Chevaillier's Strange Story. She Runs Away From the 'Primate.' Now She Vows That She Will Break Up the Licentious Community."

Thomas Lake Harris was once described by William James as "America's best-known mystic." Harris wrote numerous elegant volumes of poetry and prose in the late nineteenth century describing his complex theories of "divine marriage" and partaking of God's breath through one's own breathing.

Two of the most interesting and solidly established communes in America were founded by Harris: The first was in Brocton, New York, and the second was Fountaingrove, in Santa Rosa, California. Fountaingrove was nurtured not only by Harris's passion, intellect, and energy but also by the money and prestige of his English followers and the agricultural skill of several Japanese converts. The manorial estate still remaining at Fountaingrove testifies to the capa-

bility of Harris in managing the funds his followers provided, and the achievements in publishing, building, raising crops, and providing a new level of experience for those who lived at Fountaingrove speak well for the spirit of intelligent and industrious cooperation in the community.

At the time Alzire Chevaillier brought her charges, the Brotherhood of the New Life was practicing its peculiar principles on over seventeen hundred acres north of Santa Rosa, where it had been located for sixteen years. Community life revolved around the figure of Harris, the primate, or "pivotal man," herald of the Second Coming. Harris "was a man of slight build and moderate height, but he possessed a remarkably full chest. He had a high forehead and overhanging eyebrows denoting large perceptive faculties. His eyes had a depth so spiritual that one could easily imagine him to be in communion with the Infinite while his long beard gave him an appearance somewhat like that of the old patriarchs."[1]

Harris, born to Calvinism, traveled through Universalism, Spiritualism, and Swedenborgianism on the way to his revelation of "divine respiration," a method of breathing engendering a direct communication with God. In *The Arcana of Christianity* Harris states that a regenerated man "exercises, apparently of himself, though it is the Lord who is breathing in him, a guarded respiration. He inhales, through a Divine

19

Jane Lee Waring spent many years as a devoted follower of Harris. She became his third wife after scandals involving sex and metaphysics. (Courtesy of the Columbia University Libraries)

The spacious Victorian commandery at Fountaingrove was built to house the men of the community, but it burnt several years after its construction, in the 1890's. (Courtesy of the California State Library)

vapor, which envelops him, and which is invisible to the eye, living in this as in a protective, atmospheric sphere. This, which proceeds from him, but primarily from the Lord, is of such a quality as to repel the sin-spirits and the death-spirits who pervade the air."[2]

Sin-spirits and death-spirits, in the Harris cosmology, originate on Oriana, a destroyed planet of our own solar system, where evil was born. Evil comes to us from our moon, a piece of the exploded Oriana. Harris claimed to have voyaged to many stars and planets and described their life forms as superior to our own because they were untouched by sin. By teaching "divine respiration," he hoped to plant the seeds of a purified race on earth.

Harris was also a frequent traveler to heaven, where he had a spiritual counterpart, the Lily Queen. The idea of counterparts was crucial to his thought. "In conjugial order, upon the orderly earths of the universe, the husband takes his wife in his bosom and they are at-one, the external expression of this being the nuptial rite, never to be identified, however, with aught that is unchaste."[3] When the two beings achieve a complete intermixture of their spirits, they symbolize the Lord. Harris taught that God had two natures, masculine and feminine, and that the true name of Jesus was Jesus-Yessa, two-in-one, father-mother, including both principles. Yessa was simply the counterpart of Jesus, part of His body but invisible to others.

Harris's sexual mysticism came more and more to dominate his life. His concept of community was based on his vision of a possible relationship between men and angels and God achieved through recognition of the divine two-in-one.

Harris's first community experiment was organized in 1861 in Wassaic, New York, and included Jane Lee Waring, who was to become, many years later, Harris's third wife. By 1865 the brotherhood had enough members to require larger quarters and moved to Amenia, New York. At Amenia they were joined by Lady Maria Oliphant and her son, Laurence. The Oliphants had become interested in Harris when he was in London in 1860. Laurence's father, Sir Anthony, was a distinguished barrister. Laurence himself, before he met Harris at the age of thirty-one, had acquired considerable fame in Victorian society as a traveler, writer, diplomat, and member of parliament. His worldly success failed to satisfy his spiritual needs, however, and he abandoned everything to follow Harris. Harris immediately separated mother and son, shutting Laurence up in a barn for months, on the grounds that solitude was necessary to prepare for his new life.

The Oliphants brought to Amenia a respectable name and, even more important, enough money to enable the colony to expand once again. In 1868 Harris, with seventy-five converts to the New Life, settled in Brocton, New York. Of the years at Brocton Harris wrote:

Besides the usual operation in agriculture and vine-culture, we are engaged, first, in the wholesale pressing and shipping of hay; second, in the general nursery business; third, in the manufacture and sale of pure native wines, more especially for medicinal use. . . .

The one object of the Brotherhood is the realization of the noble Christian ideal in social service. . . . In one sense the Brotherhood are Spiritualists: in the fervid and intense conviction that the individual man has no real life in himself; that all life, and with it the virtues and energies of life, are the result of a divine inflowing. . . .

In another sense the Brotherhood are Socialists. They consider that the practical fulfillment of the Gospel is in what may be termed "Divine-natural Society."[4]

In 1875 Harris moved his community to California. The reasons for the relocation were never made clear. In an unpublished manuscript Harris recalled a former vision of himself "dwelling in the vicinage of the great forests of sequoia, near the Pacific."[5] Kanaye Nagasawa, a Japanese Christian who met Oliphant in England, came to Brocton, and remained Harris's lifelong follower, stated that the move was made because the severe eastern winters were hard on Harris's health. Harris himself wrote that staying in Brocton had caused him to become "wasted of the fine elements forming for my own new naturehood," and that the Lily Queen, in her attempts to help him, "became depleted of the substance of energy in her ultimated luminous body."[6]

At first Harris permitted only a few of his followers to come to Santa Rosa. He left even his wife in Brocton. (Harris was married to Emily Isabella Waters, a devoted spiritualist. She accepted the Lily Queen as Harris's true mate and lived in celibacy with her husband for thirty years until her death in 1885.) After a house was built, Harris sent for his wife and Miss Waring. Alice le Strange Oliphant, Laurence's wife, whom he had met and married in Europe in 1872, was called to Fountaingrove from Brocton late in 1877. Laurence himself was not summoned.

Harris often separated husbands and wives, apparently because of his belief that contact with an earthly partner would inhibit the relationship to the spiritual counterpart. (Only one married couple was ever acknowledged by Harris to be each other's counterparts, and this only after one of them died.) Laurence's marriage was permitted after Alice signed all her property over to Harris and they both agreed to remain celibate. Laurence wrote that he "learnt self-control by sleeping with my beloved and beautiful Alice in my arms for twelve years without claiming the rights of a husband."[7]

Children were also separated from their parents. "The constant prayer is for light to show us how the moral, mental and physical states of these little ones can be unfolded into the richest flowing of the Divine order. . . . Our work is to rear hero-martyrs, soldiers of the Cross, therefore they are trained to endure hardness."[8] There was little opportunity to practice these ideas, however, because there were so few children. Harris counted only five births among his

The lily pond and manor house at Fountaingrove were the setting for various communal activities. Included here are some of Harris's early Japanese followers; Kanaye Nagasawa is the second from the right. (Courtesy of the Columbia University Libraries)

The Fountaingrove winery and vineyard in 1891. This is an early setting in the history of California's wine-making tradition. Harris marketed the wine with considerable financial acumen. The occult profit from the "divine liquor" was purportedly more important than the financial profit, however. (Courtesy of the California State Library)

people in seventeen years at Brocton and Fountaingrove, although the Lily Queen bore him two spiritual children in heaven.

The Brocton community did not close its doors until 1881, when Harris called those remaining in the east to Fountaingrove. In the intervening years it was used mostly as a testing place for prospective community members.

Harris had initially bought (for $21,000) four hundred acres of the sunny wine country just north of Santa Rosa. Later he more than quadrupled his acreage. The colonists did not at first attempt to cultivate wine grapes. In its early years Fountaingrove was a dairy farm, selling its milk morning and evening in Santa Rosa, but by 1883 most of the estate had been transformed to vineyards bearing Cabernet, Pinot Noir, and zinfandel grapes. In 1886 the colony produced seventy thousand gallons of wine. Harris was pleased with this success, on both financial and spiritual grounds. He regarded community work as a religious activity and claimed that community-produced wine was infused with a divine energy.

Harris and his followers called their brotherhood the Use, a term that at first referred to each person's occupation, use, or special talent and later came to designate the entire community. The full meaning of the word was reflected in Harris's attempt to have the community members produce as many of their necessities as possible. He believed that products took on the qualities of their makers and did not wish to have his people defiled by using objects drenched in impure vibrations or his holy objects defiled by the hands of outsiders. In 1883 Harris wrote: "We are hard at work, building for the printing works. Hireling labor has become so infesting and oppressive, that we are doing the work with our own hands. What joy in labor! We shall do all the printing ourselves also; for we esteem the work too holy to be profaned by mercenary handling."[9]

One of Harris's Japanese followers, Osui Arai, did most of the typesetting for the endless stream of Harris's writing that flowed from the Fountaingrove presses. When Miss Chevaillier denounced Harris in 1891, she made special mention of Arai:

Poor Arai! He is the most abject slave of the whole colony. He works very hard in the printing-house, where he sets type, corrects proofs on the galleys, makes up the forms and runs the power press, which is operated by steam. Harris is very particular about his language in the many publications that he turns out there in the course of the year. He vacillates so much in the preparation of his matter for the press that he makes hundreds of trivial changes in the proofs and poor Arai works early and late correcting them in type. It makes the young zealot perspire but he does not complain. He says that he was taken to the community as the body servant of a wealthy Japanese who

The beautifully wrought doors of the Fountaingrove winery were handcrafted by members of the community in the 1890's. (Photograph by Paul Kagan)

was visiting California years ago. Although he has been a most devoted follower of the prophet, he has seldom seen him and is kept there by his blind, simple faith.[10]

Harris himself decided who worked at which tasks within the Use. Miss Chevaillier was shocked to find "very charming young women who were accustomed to the best society" working at servile domestic tasks. Alice Oliphant, herself a lady of gentle breeding, worked as a housekeeper during the year she spent in Santa Rosa. Laurence wrote that "she was sent away from me to toil in the humblest positions, positions which her patrician blood ill fitted her to fill."[11]

Even in the midst of keeping house, tending the vines, and milking the cows, life in the Use was never on a wholly practical level. Harris encouraged his followers to enjoy themselves ("Dance while you may, dance while you may,/For Heaven comes forth in social play"), to feel the presence of their counterparts, and to be aware of the household as a place where angels and fairies dwelt. The fairies, called fays, were described by Harris as follows:

These are, in their form, celestial-human; their varieties are numberless; their beauty exquisite, and their affections immortally infantile. . . . They indulge in the most tender caresses, one with the other, and are closely allied in their genius with the fecundating principle in plants, being frequently seen rising in the Heavens from the blossom over which they preside. . . . They delight in the endearments of conjugial associates, and sometimes single out a married pair upon the orderly earths, and, like little, sportive, aeriform children, they hive themselves within the wifely bosom, being found as well with her beloved counterpart. . . . These are the little graces of the breast.[12]

A young woman who was a member of the community wrote:

Once when I awoke I heard the strangest little noises in my breast, and everything there all day long has seemed to be in a flutter, as if little wings were moving, at least that is the nearest I can come to expressing it, and something keeps singing to me "In your breast love will build his nest." . . .

The fays have many babies, and so they keep and keep on enlarging the spaces and filling them full of beautiful houses, gardens, and groves, till at last the whole being, to the very extremities of fingers and toes, is all a fairy universe, a world of loveliness. Just think of having lovely little fays bathing in the veins.

The same young lady also provided a description of counterpartal presence:

This counterpart or something (he says that he decidedly objects to be called "or something") is keeping up such a

Members of the community at work in front of the winery in the 1890's. Note the English, American, and Japanese dress of the period. (Courtesy of Gaye LeBaron)

This double silo was used at Fountaingrove in the 1890's for the storage of materials used in the production of the "divine liquor." (Photograph by Paul Kagan)

The Fountaingrove vineyards (ca. 1890). The wine from these grapes was said to be "potentialized with the electro-Venus spirit of joy." (Courtesy of the Columbia University Libraries)

In the elysian fields of Fountaingrove in the 1890's this young woman may be contemplating Harris's complex theology of counterparts and fays. (Courtesy of Gaye LeBaron)

John Muir, the noted naturalist and conservationist, on the steps of the manor house during a visit to Fountaingrove, probably before the turn of the century. (Courtesy of Gaye LeBaron)

wonderful fluttering, stirring, rushing, and rapid movement within me. . . . I wish I could describe what this is like, somebody inside of you all over, lately it seems to be so much about my mouth and tongue, almost like a kiss.[13]

The anonymous woman's experiences were by no means unique at Fountaingrove. Mrs. Harris herself was involved in the world of the fays and gave many of them names, such as Sir Sunbeam Courage. She called herself Lady Pink-Ears and belonged to the rabbit family of fays. Her behavior, however, was regarded in the community as somewhat extreme.

The scandals that broke around Harris and ultimately forced the end of Fountaingrove as a community revolved around the counterparts and the question of whether they did or did not ever become physically manifest in somebody's bed. The first event that drew a certain amount of publicity was an attack by the Swedenborgians, who had once counted Harris

among their numbers. One of their ministers accused Harris of condoning adultery, since Harris claimed that a certain married lady accused of the sin was inhabited by the counterpart of a young man, thus rendering the act guiltless. The San Francisco *Chronicle* carried the story in the spring of 1885, and that summer a Swedenborgian periodical contained further stories of the goings-on at Fountaingrove, including married couples changing partners, naked communal bathing, and Harris himself having sexual relations with five women in a single day.

The only concrete evidence for these stories came from a visitor to the community who claimed that Miss Waring had told her that the Lily Queen would comfort her (the visitor) if she got into Mr. Harris's bed. When the visitor asked what Mr. Harris would do in such an event, she was told, "Oh, Lily Queen is inside of Father, and consequently he, of course, stays in the bed."

The sensational publicity eventually died down,

"Mr. Cowles carpentering by the Boiler House." (Courtesy of the Bancroft Library)

The bicycle mania of the 1890's even reached Fountaingrove, as is attested to by this gentlewoman on a three-wheeler. (Courtesy of Gaye LeBaron)

"Nina at lacework" (ca. 1890). (Courtesy of the Bancroft Library)

"Leno in Blacksmith Shop" (ca. 1890). (Courtesy of Gaye LeBaron)

A Japanese member at work in the gardens. (Courtesy of the Bancroft Library)

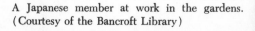

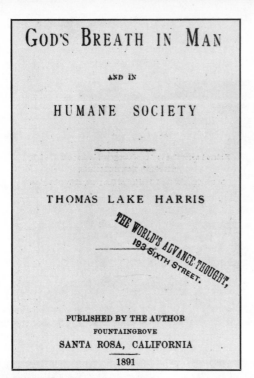

Harris published many books on diverse subjects. His philosophical system included a cosmology, metaphysics, and his own understanding of a breathing technique he called divine respiration. (Courtesy of the Huntington Library)

but then in 1891 Laurence Oliphant's cousin, Margaret Oliphant, published her *Memoir of the Life of Laurence Oliphant and of Alice Oliphant, His Wife.* Trouble with the Oliphants had begun to brew in 1878, when Harris claimed that Alice, through occult skills, had taken to making herself resemble the Lily Queen. She would then come to his bed at night, emanating "a suffocating poison, sufficient to destroy natural life."[14] Shortly thereafter Alice left Fountaingrove and never saw Harris again. She remained in California for two years, then joined her husband (who had departed Brocton for Europe), in defiance of Harris's wishes. Meanwhile, Laurence was receiving messages from the Lily Queen and from his own counterpart; Harris regarded these claims of mediumship and the contents of the communications as treason. Laurence finally felt that he had reached the end of the road with Harris and returned to America to recover as much as he could of the money he had put into the brotherhood. He had an unpleasant scene with Harris, who accused him of having gone "mediumistically insane." Laurence departed, having regained a fraction of his investment, and never returned.

The Oliphants settled in Palestine, where Alice died early in 1886, after which Laurence proclaimed

that she was his true counterpart. He married again in 1888, an act he claimed served to "draw me closer and cement more firmly my spiritual tie with Alice."[15] The marriage was ended after only four months by Laurence's death. Harris recalled his statement to Laurence when they quarreled: " 'I appeal to the tribunal of the living God for a decision between us, in the issues of life and death. If you are the criminal, you will die.' I rested calmly and left the matter there. He died."

Margaret Oliphant's book eulogized Laurence and Alice and accused Harris of immorality and financial

Laurence and Alice le Strange Oliphant came from the high society of Victorian England and Paris, bringing large sums of money to Harris's communal endeavors. Their relation to Harris, long and tempestuous, culminated with Harris accusing Laurence Oliphant of being "mediumistically insane." (Courtesy of the Columbia University Libraries and the Huntington Library)

A Fountaingrove couple. (Courtesy of Gaye LeBaron)

"Mrs. Clarke & Nina in Cottage." The cottage was the women's residence. It was also called the familistery. (Courtesy of the Bancroft Library)

One of Harris's women followers, interrupted at her reading. (Courtesy of Gaye LeBaron)

"Mr. & Mrs. Bruckner." They followed Harris, with others, from the commune at Brocton, New York. (Courtesy of the Bancroft Library)

"K. N. in the new Greenhouse." Kanaye Nagasawa was one of Harris's most devoted followers. Nagasawa's scrapbooks included photographs of John Muir and Luther Burbank visiting Fountaingrove. (Courtesy of the Bancroft Library)

Kanaye Nagasawa in 1928. At that time he was
the sole owner of Fountaingrove. When he died
in 1934, the land went to outsiders. (Courtesy
of the Columbia University Libraries)

dishonesty. The newspapers hardly had time to ex-
ploit this story when Miss Chevaillier appeared on the
scene. As a professional agitator and reformer (she
was a Christian Scientist, a nationalist, and a suf-
fragette who worked as a lecturer and journalist),
she knew how to make the most of her story. Her
understanding of the counterpart theory did the greatest damage to Harris:

After a man has been separated from his wife and has
been taken into the inner circle he is given a heavenly
counterpart, which after a time is permitted by the prophet
to descend and take material form in whatever woman he
may see fit to designate as the affinity of the disciple,
although this is, of course, all inside the community. The
condition of the morals of these people is vile.[16]

Harris was forced by the scandal into a marriage
with Miss Waring (Emily had died in 1885). Harris
was sixty-eight, and his new wife sixty-four. Following the wedding, they left Fountaingrove for New
York. Harris never returned to the Use. He died in
1906, although he had long before proclaimed himself
immortal.

After Harris's departure Fountaingrove rapidly
deteriorated as a community. In 1900 Harris sold all
his remaining interest in the property to five of the
members. The terms of the sale stipulated that the
land would remain in the hands of the one who lived
the longest and pass to his heirs. By the 1920's Kanaye
Nagasawa had become the sole owner. He kept Fountaingrove as a winery until he died in 1934. Since
Nagasawa left no family, the land went to outsiders.

The fact that the Brotherhood of the New Life and

The round barn at Fountaingrove as it looked when it was
built. It had some unique ad-
vantages in its feeding system:
"The horses approached their
stalls from various apertures and
came to a halt with their heads
in the hay and their rear ends
directly opposite an exterior
window. If this isn't perpetual
motion (provided we don't run
out of hay and horses) in the
manufacture and piling of horse
manure, I am at a loss to sug-
gest anything better" (from the
memoirs of Wallace Ware, the
son of an attorney who was a
friend of Harris, as quoted in
Gaye LeBaron's manuscript).
(Courtesy of Gaye LeBaron)

On U.S. 101 today, near Santa Rosa, the barn of the old Fountaingrove community can still be seen by passing motorists. Few people are aware of the occult origins of the round building. (Photograph by Paul Kagan)

The Fountaingrove manor house (November 24, 1912), called aestivossa by Harris, was once occupied by Harris, Emily Harris, Jane Lee Waring, Alice Oliphant, and a few select others. The furnishings were lavish and opulent. The structure contained four parlor-studies, a hand-carved staircase said to contain eighty-three original architectural concepts, a large communal dining-room, and a grand ballroom for dancing. (Courtesy of the Columbia University Libraries)

Harris's study in the manor house. Stained glass, redwood, and oak were everywhere in the building. (Courtesy of Gaye LeBaron)

The manor house at Fountaingrove, shown here during its destruction in 1970. Once it was ringed by eucalyptus trees and small gardens. Common meals were taken downstairs, and important guests were lodged upstairs. Shortly after this photograph was taken, the author found under the floorboards of the attic small bits of English lace, pencil sketches of an 1890 sea voyage across the Atlantic, and a faded, brown photograph of a Himalayan village. (Photograph by Paul Kagan)

This was the last view seen from the second floor of the manor house at Fountaingrove. Within hours the house was leveled. (Photograph by Paul Kagan)

the name of Thomas Lake Harris remain little known in American history raises a question about the actual impact of the community on the world around it. The measure of success of a communal experiment is also put to the test. In the larger perspective in which Harris viewed Fountaingrove—as "the earthly home of God's regenerating breath" and as the Noah's Ark that would survive the continuing crises of Harris's day—the buildings and institutions were to be the sole survivors of the impending doom and the seeds of a new age. Perhaps, however, the brotherhood fulfilled its purpose in the experience of its members. "In retrospect the Brotherhood may look like a bedraggled and forlorn group of utopians, yet their enterprise even now seems noble and exciting if we see them as they saw themselves and remember the long line of those who in all earnest attempted to 'live the life' of complete devotion."[17]

Herbert W. Schneider and George Lawton, authors of the definitive work on Thomas Lake Harris, *A Prophet and a Pilgrim,* observe that "the Brotherhood of the New Life resembled other better-known forms of mysticism in two respects: It was a revolt from the church for the purpose of founding a theocratic community; and it was built on an elaboration of the mythology of sex."[18] Just as Fountaingrove represented a revolt from the church, it was also a break with other traditions, and it is in this respect that it holds a common bond with the other communes studied here. They were unorthodox, and they were ephemeral.

The question of the mythology of sex is enormous. The energies of sex are so powerful and become so easily connected with fantasies that it is often difficult to differentiate between Harris's imagination, especially as revealed in the unusual sexual practices described in his theology, and what actually occurred at Fountaingrove. Even today, communal exploration of the meaning of sex goes on in group marriages, nuclear families, and so forth; the jealousies and angers generated by sexual imagination are no less today than fifty years ago. The traditional concept of transformation is often left out of sexual experimentation. Perhaps Harris understood something about the relation of sexual energy to a higher possibility for men and women, and it was this that gave his practices some short success.

Without direct participation in the process of sexual experimentation, even though it is somewhat like tampering with high-explosive devices, there is certainly very little that can be understood; the force of words on paper and the thoughts behind them rarely unite with the passion so vital to Harris's system. His sexual mysticism seems to have been the external manifestation of the changing attitudes toward sex and sexual mores at the beginning of the century. Sex was no less important for Harris than for Freud.

The title page of *Voyage en Icarie*, published in 1848. Icaria was founded on the ideals put forth in this book. (Courtesy of Ernest Marchand)

CHAPTER **3**

Icaria Speranza

Arise, worker bent in the dust!
The hour of awakening has sounded.
To the American shores, flying the banner
Of sacred community!

Soldiers of brotherhood!
Going to found in Icaria
The welfare of humanity.
　　　　　—Song of the Icarians as they left
　　　　　Le Havre on February 3, 1848

Icaria Speranza, founded in 1881 by two Frenchmen, lasted as a colony near Cloverdale, California, for only five years, but the homestead building where most of the communal activities took place still stands. The two-story white clapboard house with big porches is looted and dead. Few people realize that this was once a socialist Eden for a group of adventurous young Frenchmen. Glass from the broken windows litters the floors, and the screens are torn and rusty. Now the surrounding countryside is full of communal experiments. Young people in Sonoma County live in geodesic domes and tend organic gardens, but they know nothing of the acres of grapes, wheat, and prunes that were grown communally by the followers of the French social philosophers of 1848. The inside of the house, stripped bare by looters, gives little sense of what it must have been like originally. The large but plain rooms convey a sense of people who worked hard and lived simply. They were the last splinter group of the Icarians, whose communal groups had existed in turn in Texas, Illinois, and Iowa. Between 1881 and 1886 the fruits of their labor were tasted in their wine, which was sold in their cooperative store in Cloverdale.

After the colony disbanded, the house stood untouched and deserted for many years. Recently, however, some University of California historians came to look at it, after which word of its existence got out, and the looters came: They took the glass from the front door and then came back to take the whole door. They took the weather vane, climbing the rickety old ladder to get to it. They left only a battered lampshade and a rotting ironing board.

The grounds are overgrown with ragweed, but traces of the old garden can be seen: little white flowers near the front door steps, some daffodils, and a huge, dignified palm tree. There is a creek, still inhabited by the descendants of the snails the original colonists imported from France for eating.

An old Indian caretaker, round and toothy, is employed by the current owner of the house, a daughter-in-law of the colony's cofounder. The caretaker tried to protect the house and the sagging red barn, but the looters came anyway. "They even took the old harness we had in the barn," he says. "Hadn't been used for over thirty years. They even took that."

The colony, founded by Jules Leroux and Armand DeHay, once owned nearly nine hundred acres of land in the wine country near Cloverdale, seventy-five miles north of San Francisco. Jules Leroux and his better-known philosopher brother, Pierre, were among the disciples of Saint-Simon in France. Both brothers left their homeland following Louis Napoleon's coup d'etat in 1851. Pierre later returned to France and died there in 1871. Jules took his family to America and settled in Kansas, where he became a farmer.

Armand DeHay, a barber by trade, was married to one of Jules Leroux's daughters. DeHay was a follower of Etienne Cabet, the author of a utopian novel, *Voyage en Icarie,* published in 1848. Cabet drew ideas from Saint-Simon, Fourier, and Owen to construct his own brand of communism. Although his ideas were not original, his book was well received by French radicals, for his presentation was dramatic and imaginative.

Cabet believed man to be distinguished from animals by his reason, perfectibility, and sociability. He felt that society was poorly organized, and that inequality was the primary cause of social ills. If there could be complete equality of social rights and obligations, then true brotherhood could exist among men. He wanted to make use of contemporary developments in industry so that work in the new society would be brief, agreeable, and safe. He envisioned cities with broad streets, numerous gardens, and flower-covered islands in rivers. All transportation would be communal. Everyone would work, no one would be poor, and there would be music and dancing in the streets.

A group of his followers left for Texas in 1848, but they were ill-prepared for their venture. They were soon decimated by sickness and found themselves to be the victims of a swindling land company. Reduced in number and aspirations, they went to New Orleans to meet Cabet himself, who had just arrived. In 1849 he led them to the abandoned village of Nauvoo, Illinois, once occupied by the Mormons. Here are the words of an Icarian on the first months at Nauvoo:

No man of us has tasted of meat that year. No, nor coffee, nor fine bread. We'll be dressed in those clothes, some of silk, some of rags, which we brought into the commune; there'll be no money to buy new. Madame my wife has the robe of lace, but no shawl; I'll have five velvet waist-coats, but no shoes. Happy? Surely. We'll be making the most grand work that the world will ever see. Ah, we make mistakes, yes. And we have failed. But the plan was perfect.

For six years the colony was fairly successful. It acquired a library of six thousand volumes which

The charter and by-laws of the Icarian community located at Nauvoo, Illinois. This community was founded by Etienne Cabet himself in 1849. (Courtesy of the Huntington Library)

The buildings at Nauvoo. (Courtesy of Ernest Marchand)

was its greatest pride, found time for musical and theatrical endeavors, and published a weekly magazine. By 1855, however, it was in financial difficulty. Cabet attempted to pull things together by assuming autocratic powers, which resulted in an internal split between the "Cabetistes" and the "dissidents." The Cabetistes, who were in the minority, eventually withdrew and started a new colony near St. Louis. Cabet died in 1856, however, and the new group did not long survive him.

The Icarian community at Corning, Iowa, was founded in 1857 when the Illinois group began to weaken. (Courtesy of Ernest Marchand)

The Illinois group, weakened by the schism and by the depression of 1857, moved to Corning, Iowa, to begin again in 1860. The Civil War brought a boom in crop prices, and the Iowa Icaria was doing well by 1868. Once again there were quarrels, however, this time between young radical members and older more conservative ones. The conservative group moved about a mile to the southeast to found "New Icaria," which lasted as an agricultural community until 1898.

The more radical group, rechristened Jeune Icarie, included the Leroux and DeHay families, who were to initiate the California experiment. By 1880, when Jeune Icarie was in financial trouble and membership was declining, DeHay became interested in the possibility of once again beginning a new Icaria, this time in a more temperate climate. He emigrated to California, sent glowing accounts back to Iowa, and was soon joined in St. Helena, Napa County, by the Leroux family.

The land near Cloverdale in Sonoma County was purchased in 1881 for fifteen thousand dollars, and Icaria Speranza was born. The name Speranza came from the Leroux family: Jules's brother, Pierre, had given the title L'Esperance to a review he had founded in 1858.

The colony at first included only a few families, who immediately set to work planting acres of zinfandel grapes. Wine-making became basic to Icaria Speranza's economy, in spite of Cabet's belief in temperance. Tobacco and alcohol had been prohibited at the Illinois Icaria, but Jeune Icarie abolished these restrictions. By the end of 1882 *The Pacific Sentinel* wrote that Icaria Speranza was "destined to become one of the finest vineyards in California." The *Sentinel* further described the colony as "a rare picture of rural comfort . . . an earthly Eden." The colonists devoted a hundred acres to wheat and planned to "engage extensively in the culture of French and German prunes."

In 1883 those remaining at Jeune Icarie in Iowa decided to join the California group. With the arrival of these new members, Icaria Speranza drew up articles of agreement and made careful plans for the colony's economy. The constitutions of the earlier Icarian groups were based on three principles: the authority of the majority, the community of property, and the control of the individual by the society. Icaria Speranza's constitution included a limited admission of private property, each family being allowed to own its clothing, furniture, and household equipment, although the colony frowned on the unfettered expression of personal taste. Especially where clothing was concerned, Icaria wished to abolish fashion and sizes whenever possible.

The original Icarians from Corning, Iowa, in front of the house built by Armand DeHay in Cloverdale, ca. 1882. (Courtesy of the Huntington Library)

Icaria Speranza at Cloverdale, California, ca. 1884–1886. (Courtesy of Ernest Marchand)

An individual could receive up to fifty dollars a year in gifts from the outside. Members surrendered their other possessions to a community fund when they joined. If the fund showed a surplus at the end of a year, it was divided between the community and its members, but an individual could collect only his share if he left the community.

A system of "labor-premiums" was also instituted. All members over the age of sixteen received a premium of $1.50 for a full month of work, although the premiums were not paid if work was missed for any reason whatever. Jules Leroux was not happy with these trappings of individualism, for he felt that they violated basic socialist tenets. He also felt that the labor-premiums were not needed as an incentive to work, since there had never been a problem with shirkers.

Daily life followed a specific routine. Everyone rose with the sun, at 5 A.M. At 6:00 the men went to work, and at 9:00 the women went to work and the children to school. Work was stopped sometime between noon and 1:00, and between 2:00 and 3:00 all dined together. The hours between 3:00 and 9:00 were devoted to "enjoyments," and at 10:00 everyone went to bed.

Colony government was centered in five elected committees (works, home consumption, education, commerce, and accounts), a board of administration,

One of the 1880 outbuildings at Icaria Speranza. This shed was once used to store farm implements. (Photograph by Paul Kagan)

This was the main house at Icaria Speranza. Built in 1881, it is now an empty monument to the building style of the period. Few people seem to know of its existence or care about its preservation. (Photograph by Paul Kagan)

which handled executive matters, and a general assembly, which included every adult member and decided all questions when disagreements arose. Prospective members had to be approved by nine-tenths of the general assembly before they could be admitted, and a firm prerequisite for membership was fluency in French.

The families lived in small houses grouped around the large communal building. The Icarians believed strongly in family life and considered marriage to be a basic aspect of their community. Children were educated in the community, but with no special programs or attempts to insure their devotion to Icarian ideas. There was not much emphasis on religion. Icarians felt that they practiced Christianity by acting on the principle of brotherhood, and that ritual forms of worship were unnecessary.

Icaria Speranza had very little political contact with the outside world. Jules Leroux was strongly opposed to this withdrawal, and he attempted to disseminate his ideas through the publication of a monthly paper, called *L'Etoile du Kansas et de l'Iowa* when the colony was in the Middle West and *L'Etoile des Pauvres at des Souffrants* in California. The masthead proclaimed it to be "Organe du Communisme Libérateur des Peuples et de l'Individu." Published entirely in French, the paper included attacks on the colony itself for its failure to work with the socialist movement in the cities. The last issue appeared in 1883, just after Jules Leroux's death, and contained an obituary written by his son, eulogizing his father as a "Christian, philosopher, communist."

In spite of the colonists' original high hopes and their efforts to insure economic self-sufficiency, their aims were never achieved. They had estimated that the much higher yield of crops per acre in California would not only enable them to survive but would also give them the opportunity to engage in the scientific and literary pursuits that they valued so highly. They had further believed that by selling their Iowa land they could pay off all the debts of both colonies. The most valuable of the Iowa property and the livestock was sold without difficulty, but the rest of the land was tied up in a court case brought by some former outside donors who demanded a share in the profits from the sale. The courts eventually ordered the land to be sold, stipulating that the money realized be used to pay debts, the donors, and court costs, with any residue going to the few remaining members of Jeune Icarie. Very little ever got to Icaria Speranza, which collapsed financially in 1886. Its land was divided among the members, most of whom remained in the area and continued to farm as individuals.

Today, of the original families, only old Mrs. Armand DeHay remains on Icaria land. She is Hawaiian by birth and was married to Armand DeHay *fils*,

The old Icarian school in Cloverdale in the 1880's. The man on the left is Armand DeHay. (Courtesy of the Huntington Library)

This is the bridge in Cloverdale used by the Icarians to cross the creek that ran through their community. (Photograph by Paul Kagan)

Just as the Icarians in Corning felt the need to publish a newspaper, so did the "Young Icarians" in Cloverdale, California. (Courtesy of the Bancroft Library)

Armand DeHay *fils*, the son of Icaria's cofounder, grew to manhood at Icaria Speranza. This photograph was taken in San Francisco ca. 1910. (Courtesy of the Bancroft Library)

the son of the cofounder of Icaria Speranza. Her husband, who was born in the homestead, died recently at the age of eighty-three. Mrs. DeHay came to the area after her marriage in 1917, long after the colony had disbanded, although the school was still in operation. Her husband kept the school bell for many years after the school itself had closed its doors.

Mrs. DeHay lives in a modern ranch house, close to the freeway that cut through the old colony land in 1962 and forced her to move from an older house. There is an engraving of Pierre Leroux, Jules's philosopher brother, on her mantel—the same likeness that appears in French history books. She also displays a photograph of her father-in-law, Armand *père*, astride a horse. It was taken in 1886, just before the colony's collapse.

In Mrs. DeHay's view, Icaria Speranza was not so much an attempt to practice a political theory as an effort to establish a family colony. She does not talk about socialism; she just says they grew grapes, had a winery of which only the foundations remain, cured their own bacon, and kept chickens and rabbits. She retells her husband's story of the day he made a mistake while emptying one of the huge vats and spilled three thousand gallons of brandy into the creek, resulting in a great many drunken fish.

For her, the end of the colony meant simply that

This was the main barn, a curious product of 1880 northern California building styles. (Photograph by Paul Kagan)

Icaria Sperensa Com Jan 12 1886

A L'administration Citoyens Affin d'obtenire un reglement de comptes avec Icaria Sperensa Com, je vous déclare mon intention de me retirer, en abbandonant mes droits comme d'assosier de la dit Communauté. Votre ami. Alexis Marchand

The short life and increasing strife at Icaria in California were reflected in Alexis Marchand's 1886 letter of resignation. The letter says: "To the administration, citizens: In order to arrive at a final accord with Icaria Speranza community, I declare my intention to retire and give up my rights as an associate of the said community. Your friend. Alexis Marchand." (Courtesy of Ernest Marchand)

the land was divided among the families and then passed from parents to children. As some of the children went to the city—French Hospital in San Francisco was founded by an Icarian family—and others grew old and died, their houses and land were sold. Now she is the only one left.

Various problems seem to have contributed to the rapid demise of the colony. The economy in California in 1884 was in a slump, and this made it difficult for the Icarians to be recompensed for their efforts in the fields. The nationalistic character of the colony was a limiting factor, too, in that all the colonists were required to speak French. Although Cabet had planned for genetic control and planned parenthood in *Voyage en Icarie*, the Icarians placed their emphasis on marriage and the family instead, and individual family groups became increasingly more important than the large Icarian family. The Icarians failed to train their children in communal ideals, as was attempted at Point Loma and Llano del Rio, and no new generation came forth to carry on the communal tradition. Finally, the colony was considerably weakened by the lack of a strong and dynamic leader to carry it through times of crisis.

Factionalism had much to do with the short life span of the successive Icarian groups—starting in France and ending in California—and reflects the same problems and shortcomings faced by other socioeconomic communities, like Kaweah and Llano del Rio. Even with the sharing of possessions and the efforts toward a classless society, these groups still faced an obstacle, one that was left out of their philosophies and practices—the inner side of man. There was a naiveté in their failure to realize the fixity and strength of man's habitual ways of acting. Problems of pride, prejudice, envy, and avarice are not met simply by changing the outward forms through which these traits manifest themselves. In the case of Icaria Speranza the problem of communication was not eased by eliminating those who could not speak French, for the same arguments took place in French rather than in English. It was also necessary to understand more than the lack of communication among men—it seems that the Icarians did not recognize their own ignorance of man's possibilities. To recognize the unknown in any world-embracing scheme is a difficult problem, for it admits of the very possibility that man as he is—that is, with his ignorance of his own possibilities—cannot devise a wholly successful community plan. Of those who tried to form successful communes, often with a brave naiveté or a driven search for an alternative way of life, it would seem that the Icarians were among the least successful.

This is the porch of the abandoned main house at Icaria Speranza. Members of the community would sometimes gather here to sing French Fourierist songs after a day of working in the gardens and vineyards. (Photograph by Paul Kagan)

Mme. Helena Petrovna Blavatsky and three of the masters of the Great White Brotherhood: Kuthumi, Morya, and the Comte de Saint-Germain (Prince Ragoczy of Transylvania). This is considered an unusual picture because of the inclusion of the count. (Courtesy of the Temple of the People)

CHAPTER 4

Theosophist Communes in California

The Theosophical movement in California produced several important communes. Theosophy was already divided into factions when it entered the state, yet each of the factions was strong enough to give rise to rich and varied educational experiments in its communes. Point Loma, near San Diego, pioneered in educational innovations. Among these were the first Linotype typesetting machine for Sanskrit script and the first Greek theater in the United States for the production of lavish Greek and Shakespearean plays.

Krotona, first in Hollywood and later in Ojai, attracted writers, artists, translators, and inventors. If a cultural influence can be felt in Hollywood that precedes the movie industry, it comes in part from Krotona's quasi-Oriental architectural forms. Besides Point Loma and Krotona, there is another, smaller offshoot of Theosophy—the aging community of Halcyon, or Temple of the People—near Pismo Beach, not far from Santa Barbara. The Varian brothers, Russell and Sigurd, who pioneered in the field of nuclear electronics and the development of the klystron tube, introduced around the time of the Second World War, were raised in Halcyon. Another of Halcyon's members (and a founder as well), Dr. William H. Dower, gave the first demonstration of an X-ray machine in California, at the Halcyon sanatorium in 1906.

In the arts, the sciences, social services, and educa-

tion, these Theosophical communities contributed much to the history of California. What was Theosophy, and what did it have to do with these groups of people who called themselves Theosophists? Did their philosophy accomplish for them psychologically what it seems to have manifested in outer accomplishments?

I. THEOSOPHICAL BACKGROUND

In 1873 Mme. Helena Petrovna Blavatsky came to New York from Paris, drawn by her interest in spiritualist phenomena, which she wished to observe and report as a journalist. At a séance she met Col. Henry Steel Olcott, who shared her interest. The popular appeal of spiritualism in America was already past its peak, but H.P.B. (as she is usually referred to by Theosophists) and Col. Olcott gathered a handful of followers and in 1875 formed a society dedicated to the exploration of spiritualism and the occult. The founders of the Theosophical Society vowed to teach an ancient esoteric wisdom, oppose all forces of materialism, and work toward the brotherhood of man.

As H.P.B.'s interests shifted, the emphasis on spiritualism was gradually replaced by the doctrines of karma and reincarnation, still the twin pillars of Theosophical thought. Although most later Theosophists rejected the exploration of occult phenomena such as clairvoyance or telekinesis, H.P.B. was very much in touch with the spiritual world. She was always complaining of unruly elementals (subhuman astral spirits) tugging at her skirts and demanding attention. It is reported that once she ordered them to hem some towels, as she was a poor seamstress; she put the towels in a cupboard, shut the door, and removed them an hour later, badly hemmed.

H.P.B.'s *Isis Unveiled*, published in 1877, contained material she claimed to have received directly from masters of the Great White Brotherhood in Tibet during her early wanderings. These masters wished to use her as a means of reaching Western peoples. The masters, or adepts, of the Great White Brotherhood are believed to be men who voluntarily remain in a physical body even though they are sufficiently evolved to escape the cycle of reincarnations. Their purpose is to aid humanity in fulfilling God's plan. H.P.B. spoke of several masters, including ones who had formerly inhabited the bodies of Pythagoras, Plotinus, and Christ. Although at least one critic claimed that he had found the source of all her material in previously published occult works, her book provided an impressive text for the new society.

In 1878 H.P.B. left America for England and India, accompanied by Col. Olcott. She attracted prominent followers in her travels, but she also drew further charges of plagiarism, which damaged her reputation somewhat. In 1884 she was accused by two recently dismissed employees at her new headquarters in Adyar, India, of instructing them in how to fake psychic phenomena. This led to her denunciation by the British Society for Psychical Research "as one of the most accomplished, ingenious, and interesting impostors in history," a judgment that proved almost ruinous. She continued to control the society, however, and published *The Secret Doctrine* in 1888. She also managed to attract the brilliant and well-known intellectual Annie Besant, friend and colleague of George Bernard Shaw and Susan B. Anthony, to Theosophy.

When H.P.B. died in 1891, there was the inevitable struggle over succession between Col. Olcott in India and William Quan Judge, a charter member who had led the society in America during H.P.B.'s absence. Annie Besant threw her support first one way and then the other, finally joining Olcott in Adyar and attempting to force Judge's resignation through a charge that he had forged a letter from a master. Most American Theosophists were loyal to Judge, however; they finally withdrew from the Adyar organization and formed their own society, with Judge

After Mme. Blavatsky left the United States, William Quan Judge managed the American Theosophical movement. With his accession to the leadership in 1891, the various schisms in the movement began. (Courtesy of Betty Warrington)

Katherine Tingley, founder of Point Loma, "wearing the ring which Helena Petrovna Blavatsky wore as the seal of her office; which she gave to William Quan Judge when she made him her successor, and which Katherine Tingley received from William Quan Judge by right of succession to him." (Courtesy of Emmett Greenwalt)

as president. Adyar continued to operate its own lodges in America, and the schism was never mended.

Judge died in 1896, within a year of the formation of the new American society, and Katherine Tingley, a remarkable woman who had met Judge in the last years of his life, took control. Mrs. Tingley, sometimes called the Purple Mother because of her fondness for that color, was in her forties, childless though thrice-married, and a former philanthropist and do-gooder. Theosophy had appealed to her because of its doctrines of karma and reincarnation, which seemed to answer the question she constantly confronted in her philanthropic work: Why are some people rich and strong and others poor and weak? She had also been interested in spiritualism and had displayed certain mediumistic powers. Although a relative newcomer, she convinced the society that Judge spoke through her, and she skillfully used this occult credential to gain control. All but a few followed her. One small group claimed to have received instructions from the Great White Brotherhood not to accept Mrs. Tingley's leadership and built its own community, Halcyon, while Mrs. Tingley created her domed city several hundred miles farther south at Point Loma.

Thus at the close of the nineteenth century there were at least three groups in the United States calling themselves Theosophists. All claimed descent from H.P.B., but they were divided by allegiance and geography. One group still looked to the East, to Adyar, but the other two focused on the West, spe-cifically California, where many of their number thought the new race would be born.

II. POINT LOMA

Katherine Tingley had a vision of an ideal community, a white city in the West where Theosophy could be lived and a new generation prepared in a special way to lead the world toward brotherhood. A true autocrat, she did not plan to let her community be governed socialistically—she intended to own its property and set its policies herself.

Mrs. Tingley set off in 1896 with a group of followers on a worldwide crusade for Theosophy. She toured Europe, Egypt, and even the Olcott-Besant stronghold of India. She had little success in drawing Indian Theosophists to her, but she claimed to have made contact with one of H.P.B.'s masters in the Himalayas, and some considered her crusade worthwhile on this count alone. Meanwhile, steps were being taken to realize her plans for a community at Point Loma, which she had never actually seen. Her representatives purchased 132 acres there, adjacent to a U.S. military base, while she was abroad. On her return she visited Point Loma, inspected her land with its magnificent view, laid a cornerstone there in February, 1897, with her characteristic ceremony, and went off on a tour of the United States.

Mrs. Tingley spent the next two years gaining absolute control of her society. She changed its name

When Mrs. Tingley returned from her worldwide crusade for Theosophy in 1897, she inspected her southern California property and laid a cornerstone at Point Loma. Dressed in a purple robe, she sprinkled corn, oil, and wine on the stone and proclaimed it "a perfect square, a fitting emblem of the perfect work that will be done in the temple for the benefit of humanity and the glory of the ancient sages." (Courtesy of the San Diego Public Library)

to The Universal Brotherhood and Theosophical Society and wrote a new constitution giving her power for life. She then became involved in Spanish-American War relief and went to Cuba in 1899, where she established connections that she later used in bringing Cuban children to her school at Point Loma. Although far from Point Loma, she did not forget it but made plans to hold the Theosophical congress there that year. This was accomplished with the pageantry she loved—trumpets were blown, flags raised, invocations chanted, and *The Eumenides* was performed, with two hundred in the cast. The San Diego newspapers were greatly impressed.

The big buildings had begun to go up at Point Loma in 1898. In 1900 the hotel-sanatorium was domed with aquamarine glass, the temple with Mrs. Tingley's favorite purple. The immense domes glittered with the reflected light of the sun; at night they were illuminated from within. On top of the domes were ornamental glass spheres, creating an architecture noticeable even in southern California. Offices, homes, and cottages for the pupils in Mrs. Tingley's new school were also constructed. One wealthy member built a home for himself with a spiral staircase outside and a nine-hole golf course in the backyard.

Point Loma welcomed visitors, and a sampling of their impressions is a tribute to Mrs. Tingley's efforts, in her own phrase, to make the community "Theosophy in practice":

The doctor, the dentist, and the plumber, the linotype operator in the print shop, and the engineer in the power plant, were all working without wages, working hard, and, as far as I could see, very happy at their tasks. It was somewhat difficult to adjust one's mind to such conditions. [A journalist, 1907][1]

I thought I was transported to ancient Greece, with its beautiful temples and balmy air. When I saw these beautiful young girls dancing, with their sandals and garlands, so like the ancient Greeks, I said again, "What spot is this? Am I standing on the Acropolis of Athens?" [A Japanese dignitary, 1909]

I do not need to be told what is going on here. I feel it in the unison of voices, in the faces, the gestures and the tones, I see it in the harmony that prevails everywhere, which permeates the atmosphere, which vibrates in all of you; and these vibrations make me think that you are keeping step with the heart-beats of God. [A professor from Columbia University, 1917]

The Raja-Yoga School was the most important experiment undertaken at Point Loma. "Let me have a child from the time of birth until it is seven years old, and all the temptation in the world will not move it,"

Point Loma, ca. 1910. The hotel-sanatorium is at the far right, and the temple is center right. The seats at the lower left are part of the Greek theater. The inset at the lower right is the Roman gate, which was the main entrance to Point Loma. (Courtesy of Iverson L. Harris)

The Photo and Engraving Department at Point Loma, where young students learned to be masters of their craft. (Courtesy of the California Western University Library)

"Raja-Yoga boys receiving tuition in presswork at the Aryan Theosophical Press." From these presses many of the fine Point Loma publications were issued. (Courtesy of the Bancroft Library)

This 1911 cover of *The Theosophical Path* was designed by a Point Loma member, Reginald Machell. The magazine was also published in Swedish, Dutch, German, and Spanish. (Courtesy of the Bancroft Library)

said Mrs. Tingley, paraphrasing the Jesuits. She believed that what she called the lower nature could be overcome through the proper teaching of self-control, beginning as early in life as three years. When a child had a temper tantrum, he was shown his face in a mirror and told that when he saw himself smile, his higher nature would again be in control. *Raja-Yoga* means "kingly union" and signifies an attempt to bring all the faculties into balance.

The school started in 1900 with a few children, but its students grew to three hundred within ten years. The children were divided into small groups under a teacher who stayed with them at all times. They lived together in cottages with pointed roofs and skylights, with flowers all around, and were permitted to see their parents for only two hours on Sunday afternoon. Formal classroom instruction never lasted more than three hours each day, but these hours were used with great efficiency. Raja-Yoga students impressed visitors with their ability in spelling, arithmetic, music, and other subjects, and many Raja-Yoga teaching methods were much later adopted in the California public schools.

The children averaged, perhaps, five years old, but the problems they solved were something like this:

Six times 3, one half, one third, times 4 plus 3, one-fifth, times 10 plus 10 plus 10 plus 50 plus 44 square root equals what? Every eye was fixed on the teacher and the answer came promptly every time, first from one child, then from another. . . .

Here were these young people shut away from the world: I wondered whether they knew anything at all of its life and its problems. So I suggested that I should like to hear about the most discussed public question of the day—that of railroad regulation in the United States. . . . A boy of fourteen gave it as his conviction that the fundamental difficulty in the railroad problem (and, he added, in politics) was the suspicion and selfishness of men![2]

Outside the classroom children worked in the gardens (which yielded more than 123,000 pounds of fruit in a single year) or in one of the community industries, practiced their music, and played games. Sometimes the schedule was interrupted for work on one of Point Loma's elaborate dramatic presentations. Through it all a rule of silence was maintained, with all but essential conversation outlawed, since the Purple Mother believed that silence fed the soul.

Mrs. Tingley concentrated so much of her energy and resources in Point Loma that the Theosophy movement in the rest of the country suffered a great deal. Most of the lodges organized by Judge were disbanded, and many disheartened members went over

Raja-Yoga tots in military regalia (January, 1903). This was taken shortly after the Spanish-American War, and patriotism was running high. (Courtesy of the San Diego Public Library)

Journalist Ray Stannard Baker remarked on the "paralyzing dignity" displayed by the Raja-Yoga children: "Sitting at their tables . . . with singular quietude, even the little children gave the appearance of absorbed occupation." Throughout their activities a rule of silence was maintained (January 7, 1903). (Courtesy of the San Diego Public Library)

Point Loma possessed a full orchestra, composed of older students and members of the community. (Courtesy of the University of California at San Diego)

As part of their formal education, younger children (four to six years old) were thoroughly instructed in music. In this photograph, taken about 1906, Judith Tyberg is the teacher. (Courtesy of Iverson L. Harris)

Dr. Tyberg today runs the East-West Cultural Center in Los Angeles. She is an accomplished scholar and a student of Sri Aurobindo. (Photograph by Paul Kagan)

A joyful moment on the beach.
(Courtesy of the California
Western University Library)

The first Greek theater in America,
erected by the Point Loma Theosophists in 1901, as it looked in
1912. (Courtesy of Iverson L.
Harris)

to the Adyar Theosophists. Mrs. Tingley drew much criticism for closing the lodges and also for her autocratic behavior in general.

The Raja-Yoga School was also attacked by the New York Society for the Prevention of Cruelty to Children, through whose influence eleven Cuban children en route to Point Loma were denied entry to the country in 1902. The ridiculous testimony against Point Loma included accusations that Mrs. Tingley called her spaniel The Purple Inspiration (although she claimed he was just "Spot"), taught children that plants marry and have babies, and required children to stand and say, "We like our lotus mother and are glad to be here" for visitors. More seriously, perhaps, she was also accused of considering herself a second Christ. The press enjoyed itself over all this, but Mrs. Tingley and her school were ultimately vindicated by inspectors from a California chapter of the S.P.C.C. and by Commissioner General Frank P. Sargent, of the U.S. Bureau of Immigration, who visited Point Loma and were favorably impressed by what they saw. The Cuban children were released and arrived triumphantly at the school.

Mrs. Tingley believed that the Adyar Theosophists were behind this trouble, and she staged a swift, vicious, and damaging counterattack on them by exploiting her knowledge that the Adyar leader in America, Alexander Fullerton, was a homosexual. When the parents of a boy seduced by Fullerton brought their son, complete with incriminating letters, to Point Loma to be reformed, she had the evidence she needed. She sent the letters to the New York Society for the Suppression of Vice, and Fullerton was arrested, judged insane, and committed to a mental institution.

In later years, when Annie Besant's colleague, C. W. Leadbeater, was accused of homosexuality, Mrs. Tingley had members of her organization picket meetings of the Adyar Theosophists and distribute leaflets denouncing the Adyar society as an abode of vice. One pamphlet, titled *Mrs. Annie Besant and the Moral Code*, included an introduction by Kenneth Morris, a Welsh poet and long-time Point Loma resident: "We must have brave men who will go in, and handle filth and breathe stench, because humanity is threatened. . . . Mr. Leadbeater, posing as an initiate . . . had been teaching boys, under pledge of secrecy, a private vice; Mrs. Besant has stood by, endorsed and defended him. . . . Is it not time to take action?"

The pamphlet quoted a circular distributed in America by Fullerton: " 'X. [Leadbeater] admitted the facts and explained that he taught masturbation to boys as a protection against relations with women.

In the Greek theater (1911): "Tableau: Socrates and his Disciples, from 'The Aroma of Athens,' Athenian Flower Festival, presented in the open-air Greek Theatre." (Courtesy of Iverson L. Harris)

Mrs. Besant utterly repudiated such doctrine and such practice, but considered X.'s motive as sincere.' " Other Adyar literature was also effectively used in the case against Leadbeater: " 'Now it was most easy for Mr. Leadbeater with clairvoyant vision to see what thought-forms were hovering about certain boys, . . . Hence the "crime" or "wrong" of teaching the practice alluded to was no crime or wrong at all, but only the advice of a wise teacher.' "

The scandal did force Leadbeater's resignation from the Adyar society, but he remained close to Mrs. Besant, who became president of the Adyar society at Olcott's death in 1907. She later reinstated Leadbeater, in spite of the fact that members of her own lodges complained that Leadbeater was known to have taught masturbation when he was still an Anglican priest. An English magazine (*John Bull*, February 6, 1909) expressed its fears that Mrs. Besant's society was "gathering into its ranks an army of morbid moral degenerates, whose teachings are calculated to undermine the character and sap the manhood of our race." At Point Loma this article was read with interest.

Katherine Tingley also did battle with the Los Angeles *Times*, which accused her of starving the children in her care and permitting "gross immorali-

"Raja-Yoga students as Flower-Girls in Katherine Tingley's production of
the ancient Greek Mystery-Drama, 'The Eumenides' of Aeschylus" (ca.
1910). (Courtesy of Iverson L. Harris)

ties" among her "disciples of spookism." She sued for libel. The *Times'* counsel tried to distract the jury from the fact that the charges could not be proved. He asked Mrs. Tingley if people at Point Loma were sun worshipers, and in his final appeal to the jury he claimed that "Christian civilization is at stake." This risk was taken; Mrs. Tingley won and was awarded $7,500.

The colony prospered for many years and pursued its principles without further harassment, but by the mid-1920's its fortunes had considerably declined. Point Loma was always financially dependent on members' contributions; the school realized some profit, but none of the other projects were self-supporting. The tremendous expenses were often greater than the colony's income. Many lodges around the country had closed, and their former members went to the Adyar organization with their money. Several years earlier a one-time strong supporter of Mrs. Tingley had defected and founded the United Lodge of Theosophists, which was successful enough to draw even more from Point Loma's resources. Mrs. Tingley was

forced to rely more and more exclusively on a few wealthy backers, and her expectations were often disappointed. Finally, in 1927, with Point Loma deeply in debt, some of the land was mortgaged, which sufficiently met the crisis for colony life to continue on its usual scale.

Mrs. Tingley made a trip to Europe in 1929 and never returned. She was injured in an automobile accident, and although the injuries were not fatal, she was by then eighty-two and already in ill health. She retired to her bed, and issuing orders to the last, refused to be moved to a hospital in spite of her doctor's insistence. She died six weeks later.

Mrs. Tingley was succeeded by Dr. Gottfried de Purucker, who had been with her since 1896. De Purucker dropped "Universal Brotherhood" from the title of his organization, changed the name of the Raja-Yoga School to Lomaland School, and waived the rule of silence. He also attempted to mend the rift with Adyar but did not wholly succeed. This was a serious disappointment, since Adyar had money, and money was once again badly needed.

A scene from *A Midsummer Night's Dream*. At Point Loma practical children were encouraged to be artistic, and artistic children were encouraged to be practical. This was part of an effort to bring all the faculties into balance. (Courtesy of Judith Tyberg)

"After the Gypsy Dance," a spectacular feature introduced by Katherine Tingley in her production of *As You Like It.* "In the Gypsy life you read / The Life that all would like to lead." (Courtesy of Iverson L. Harris)

De Purucker died suddenly in 1942. The Theosophists had left Point Loma a few months earlier in the same year. Community affairs had economically deteriorated immediately following Katherine Tingley's death and the stock-market crash of 1929. The military base adjoining Point Loma had become strategic, noisy, and undesirable as a neighbor. It was not until 1945 that the society announced the selection of a new president, Col. A. L. Conger, who remained in office until his death in 1951. At that time the society was split again when James A. Long, a man unacceptable to some Point Loma Theosophists, became president.

James Long did not believe that Point Loma had a place in the history of California communes. He did not view it as a utopian experiment but as a school, one small turn in the Theosophists' path. "Any image of a communal or utopian group was manufactured completely by people outside the ranks of the Society and was an incorrect label."[3]

Although Long claimed until he died in 1971 that his organization was the only one "through which the White Lodge works," a number of long-time Theosophists handed in their resignations when Long took control. Iverson L. Harris, who left to start his own Point Loma Publications, wrote to the society: "Please strike my name off your list of members. . . . I have trust in a Higher Law and am confident that life-long consecration to the Theosophical Movement on the part of any earnest student is duly recorded

on the Screen of Time. So, also, is ruthless disregard of basic Theosophical principle—sometimes, alas, coupled with blasphemy of the Masters' names."

In 1965 Harris and his first wife, Helen, donated their considerable inclusive library to the University of California at San Diego. In more recent years he has assembled another library, mainly of Theosophical books, magazines, and archives. He has written and published several books, including *The Wisdom of Confucius, The Wisdom of Laotse, Theosophy under Fire,* and *Mme. Blavatsky Defended.* The last was advertised as a "Refutation of Falsehoods, Slanders, and Misrepresentations Published by The National Broadcasting Company, Truman Capote, Walter Winchell, The John Birch Society, Time Magazine, and Others." (Theosophists of every stripe were particularly outraged at *Time's* linking H.P.B. with Sirhan Sirhan's assassination of Senator Robert F. Kennedy.[4])

Another Point Loma Theosophist who refused to follow James Long is Dr. Judith Tyberg, who entered the Raja-Yoga School when she was four days old and lived in the community most of her life:

I was there for forty-four years, and then I left—some wrong people got in at the head, and their ideals were absolutely not up to the way we had been brought up, and so a lot of us just left. . . . They began dismissing people from this and that who had been there for years and years. . . . The thing's just gone to nothing, nothing now, just a few old people living together. . . . Oh, my whole heart was Theosophy! Absolutely! And then come these little upstarts with no background or dedication or learning or culture and take over.[5]

Dr. Tyberg now runs the East-West Cultural Center in Los Angeles and devotes herself particularly to the work of Sri Aurobindo.

The Theosophists who remained in the organization set up by Mrs. Tingley moved from Point Loma to Covina and then to Altadena, which is still their headquarters. They own a very large and elaborately furnished house on spacious, well-tended grounds, but it is not a real community any more. The residents are few and not young. Two of the women were students in the Raja-Yoga School many years ago. One is old and soft and mellow, the other middle-aged and slightly brittle; but both are gracious, clear-eyed, and happy to recall their school days. The older woman's parents were Theosophists in William Quan Judge's day.

They emphasize the creative aspects of their Raja-Yoga education, the study of arts and crafts and music.

Mrs. Tingley believed in the beneficent effects of music:

The soul power which is called forth by a harmony well delivered and well received does not die away with the conclusion of the piece. It has elicited a response from within the nature, the whole being has been keyed to a higher pitch of activity, and even the smallest of daily duties, those which are usually called menial, will be performed in a different way, upon a higher plane, as a result.

The goal of bringing all the faculties into balance was implemented by encouraging artistic children to do practical things, and practical children to do artistic things. The ideal of brotherhood was pursued by teaching even the smallest children to think of others first. The students were from many backgrounds, and the school did not tamper with any previous religious training they had received. Theosophy, however, was in the air, personified by Mrs. Tingley, who was regarded as mother, teacher, and healer, someone who knew how to make people well. The students did not

Point Loma at its zenith, ca. 1915. Few of the buildings remain today. One of them, the temple, was destroyed by fire; another, the academy, was removed as a safety hazard in the 1950's. (Courtesy of Iverson L. Harris)

think of her as dictatorial, but they never questioned her absolute authority.

The remaining Theosophists at Altadena still seem to be waiting for a Theosophical revival in the world; they stand by their belief in an active brotherhood among men, even though few listen any more. Their Theosophical University, organized in 1919, is inactive, "in abeyance" they say, although legally still in existence. Public meetings ended ten or fifteen years ago. An Australian convert is cataloging the library, where a forbidding portrait of H.P.B. is promi- nent. The rooms are full of Oriental rugs and ancient Chinese ivory carvings and pottery, original manu- scripts of Mozart and Handel, and furniture created by Point Loma's most famous artist, Reginald Machell. In the midst of these amazing treasures the Australian insists that Theosophy is not concerned with outer forms, and that it is contradictory to look for the tangible remains of spiritual endeavors. He admits that what is left at Point Loma may help whatever is there now to grow in its own way.

The Theosophists maintain a print shop with a

Point Loma's elegant Victorian furnishings, replete with ancient Chinese carvings and Oriental rugs, as seen in an administration building, ca. 1910. (Courtesy of Iverson L. Harris)

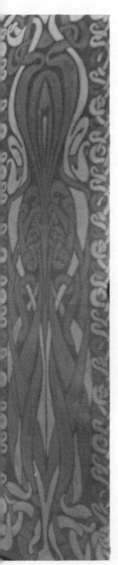

fairly new offset press but very old Linotype and cutting machines a short distance from the house at Altadena. Here they produce their beautifully printed monthly magazine, *Sunrise,* as well as Theosophical books. H.P.B. is still read, and Theosophical University Press editions of *Isis Unveiled* and *The Secret Doctrine* produce some income.

Point Loma itself is now the campus of Point Loma College, affiliated with the Church of the Nazarene. There is a Theosophical scrapbook in the library, filled with pictures of fantastically costumed players in the lavish Point Loma Greek and Shakespearean

"Mrs. Tingley's bedroom on the second floor of Head-quarters. Over the head of her bed hung the painting of 'The Master of Vibrations'. A pongee curtain hid it. At her instructions, Dixie was rocked for a time every day." Theosophists of every faction were strong in the anti-vivisection movement. (Courtesy of the San Diego Public Library)

A Japanese commercial commission visiting Point Loma, with Mrs. Tingley as hostess. (Courtesy of Iverson L. Harris)

Dr. Gottfried de Purucker became Mrs. Tingley's successor in 1929 and directed Point Loma until his death in 1942. (Courtesy of Iverson L. Harris)

Katherine and Grace Knoche, Jr., were both born at Point Loma. They are shown here as young girls during the early heyday of the community. (Courtesy of Iverson L. Harris)

productions. There are also postcards with photographs of clean and shiny young faces, with captions like "Raja Yoga tots going to school so happy and bright," "Tiny lotus buds," and "I love the Raja Yoga school." There is a picture of "a cow that gives milk for the Raja Yoga babies" and even one of Katherine Tingley's famous pet dog, Spot. The scrapbook also includes propaganda material and cartoons concerning Mrs. Tingley's favorite crusades, most notably antivivisection and prison reform. She was strongly opposed to capital punishment and was instrumental in preventing the execution of at least one condemned murderer.

The huge domed temple and most of the other original Point Loma buildings are gone, although the Greek theater remains, with a plaque reading "First Greek Theater in America. Built A.D. 1901 by the Universal Brotherhood and Theosophical Society under leadership of Katherine Tingley. The Society occupied these premises from 1897 to 1942." The classic lines of the theater are pure, and the view is magnificent, but it is not the same. The land behind the theater once dropped straight away to the ocean; now the canyon has been filled, and basketball courts and baseball diamonds are neatly laid out between the pillars and the sea.

Katherine Knoche Macdonald and Iverson Harris, both Point Loma alumni, married in 1972. Harris today presides over an active Theosophical nonprofit educational and religious corporation called Point Loma Publications, Inc. (Photograph by Paul Kagan)

This unusual spiral staircase, now in ruins, once supported a glass dome that covered the Albert G. Spalding house at Point Loma. Now the steps lead nowhere, and they present a visual anomaly among the modern buildings of Point Loma College, sponsored by the Church of the Nazarene. (Photograph by Paul Kagan)

The Halcyon sanatorium as it looked in 1904. Having rejected the leadership of Katherine Tingley, the Temple of the People acquired the sanatorium and about a hundred acres of land in Oceano. (Courtesy of the Temple of the People)

The assembled 1916 annual convention of the Temple Home Association in front of the sanatorium. Francia LaDue, "Blue Star," is seated in the left center foreground, wearing a white robe, and Dr. William H. Dower, "Red Star," is immediately to the left. (Courtesy of Dorothy Varian)

An early copy of *The Temple Artisan*, Halcyon's journal devoted to science, philosophy, mysticism, and the arts. It is still being published quarterly today, with the same front-cover format. (Courtesy of the Temple of the People)

III. HALCYON

Only one-half of the inhabitants of Halcyon today are Theosophists, although at one time the entire community was a Theosophical venture. The Theosophists of Halcyon are a splinter group. For a group so small, their influence in California has been considerable. A number of prominent intellectuals were drawn to Halcyon, including friends and co-workers of Upton Sinclair (who attempted to utilize the Theosophical vote in his unsuccessful campaign for governor).

The Halcyon Theosophists arrived in California from Syracuse, New York in 1903, led by Dr. William H. Dower and Mrs. Francia LaDue. Their journey resulted from the schism in the Theosophical Society following Katherine Tingley's rise to power in 1896. Dr. Dower and Mrs. LaDue believed that in rejecting Mrs. Tingley's leadership they were carrying on the true work of the Theosophists in a direct line from Mme. Blavatsky.

They acquired about a hundred acres of land, organized themselves as the Temple Home Association, and concentrated their work in a sanatorium purchased and run by Dr. Dower, which opened in 1904. It is a forbidding yellow Victorian mansion that stands near the ocean, a couple of miles from the Temple of the People. The temple itself was built by

The Temple Artisan

JULY, 1903

CONTENTS

	PAGE
THE HARP OF INFINITY	17
THE LESSON OF THE ROSES, *B. S.*	18
ASTROLOGY, *Florence A. Barnett*	19
ENERGY OF REFLECTION AND REFRACTION	21
EDITORIAL MIRROR	23
LETTERS FROM MANILA, *John W. Cleave*	25
THE LETTER BOX	28
WHERE DID IT GO? *W. E. Gannet*	30
THE AWAKENING OF THE SOUL *Maeterlinck*	31
TEMPLE ACTIVITIES AND NOTICES	31

Mysticism, Social Science and Ethics

PUBLISHED AT
OCEANO, CALIFORNIA

Price 10 Cents $1.00 Per Year

The officers of the Halcyon temple shortly after its completion in the early 1920's. In the foreground are John Varian and Dr. William H. Dower. From left to right at the top are Jane Dower (who married the doctor after a minor uproar among the temple membership), Mrs. Wilkins, Ernest Harrison, and Agnes Varian. All were early members of the Halcyon community. (Courtesy of the Temple of the People)

John and Agnes Varian in front of their home at Halcyon about 1930. John Varian was an Irish poet, a musical experimentalist, and the father of Russell and Sigurd Varian, who invented the klystron tube. (Courtesy of Dorothy Varian)

Inside the Varian house in 1932, Agnes rocks in front of a harp that was built as part of one of John's musical experiments. (Courtesy of Dorothy Varian)

Mrs. Linda Rollison and her son Damian were residing in the old Varian house in 1971 as members of the Halcyon Theosophist community. Many others had lived in this house since the Varians. (Photograph by Paul Kagan)

"Taken by Maude J. Wilson. About 1910. Mr. Webber? Baker at Halcyon." (Courtesy of the Temple of the People)

the members in 1923–1924 from cement blocks made from the gravel found in the nearby creek.

The Temple Home Association was run along socialist lines: "All the land will be owned all of the time by all of the people; all the means of production and distribution, tools, machinery and natural resources, will be owned by the people—the Community; and Capital and Labor may meet on equal terms with no special privileges to either."[6] Many of the early Theosophists were also utopians of the Edward Bellamy school, and many later embraced the brand of socialism presented by men like Upton Sinclair. Each member received living expenses, a small monthly salary, and half an acre to farm on his own.

Financial difficulties eventually forced the end of the venture as a cooperative colony, but the temple is still active. Harold E. Forgostein, the current guardian-in-chief of the temple, tells visitors about the similarities between Theosophy and other religions, the importance of the golden rule, and the price humanity is paying for its failure to follow it. He believes that the exploration of psychic phenomena is destructive because it "has no spiritual significance [and] leads to unbalance, even insanity."

Forgostein talks about the temple as the only one

The temple was begun in 1923, built of cement blocks made from the gravel found in the nearby creek. (Courtesy of the Temple of the People)

Dr. Dower, photographed while watching the construction of the triangle-shaped temple in 1924. (Courtesy of the Temple of the People)

The completed Halcyon temple, with Dr. Dower and Mrs. LaDue in the left foreground wearing dark clothing. (Courtesy of Dorothy Varian)

The Halcyon Temple of the People as it looks today. Harold E. Forgostein is the current guardian-in-chief of the temple. (Photograph by Paul Kagan)

Francia LaDue, a founding leader of Halcyon. (Courtesy of the Temple of the People)

in the direct line of succession through Blavatsky and Judge. "Tingley was wrong," he says. "Our temple has direction from the masters." The temple has no connection with any other Theosophical organization. Many Besant and Tingley Theosophists have never heard of Halcyon. There is no publicity-seeking and no attempt to recruit new members. The small Halcyon community cemetery is dominated by the graves of Dr. and Mrs. Dower and Mrs. LaDue.

The Sanatorium, still affectionately called the San, now serves in incongruous dignity as the office for a trailer court. It was once surrounded by tall trees, but they were all cut down to make room for the trailers in the eight years since the building was sold.

Only a few of the old grave-markers are legible today in the Halcyon cemetery. Among them are those of Dr. and Mrs. Dower and Francia LaDue, all guardians-in-chief of the Temple of the People. Temple members today are interred in the same grounds. (Photograph by Paul Kagan)

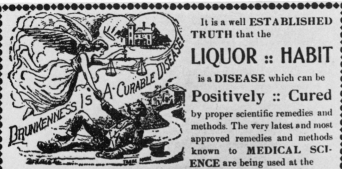

It is a well **ESTABLISHED TRUTH** that the

LIQUOR :: HABIT

is a **DISEASE** which can be

Positively :: Cured

by proper scientific remedies and methods. The very latest and most approved remedies and methods known to **MEDICAL SCIENCE** are being used at the

Halcyon :: Sanatorium

in curing the **Liquor, Opium and Morphine Habits** and all diseases caused by the same. All appetite and desire for liquor and narcotics is **thoroughly eradicated**; shattered nerves restored to normal tone, and the entire system **rejuvenated** by the remedies and healing forces so successfully employed at this institution, which, though only opened to the public a year ago, has already earned a high reputation, far and wide, for its successful work. For additional information and terms, address

THE HALCYON SANATORIUM, Oceano, Calif.

Dr. Dower brought fame and sometimes notoriety to Halcyon through his treatment of alcoholics and addicts at the sanatorium. This ad is from a 1906 *Temple Artisan*. (Courtesy of the Bancroft Library)

Herman Volz in 1971. He arrived at Halcyon with his mother and his sister in July, 1920. Mr. Volz is the scribe of the Temple of the People. He is also a fine gardener, and he works with the water supply. (Photograph by Paul Kagan)

Richard Lentz, the postmaster at Halcyon in 1971. The recent store sign that graces the old building is indicative of some youthful interest in Halcyon today. (Photograph by Paul Kagan)

The old sanatorium was the first building acquired by the Halcyon Theosophists. The community sold it some years later, and it is now the headquarters of a trailer camp. (Photograph by Paul Kagan)

IV. KROTONA

Krotona—the name comes from Crotona, Italy, home of the Pythagorean School—is the California outpost of the Adyar Theosophists, the largest and best-organized surviving Theosophical group. Branches exist in more than fifty countries. The United States national headquarters are in Wheaton, Illinois.

Krotona was founded in Hollywood in 1912 by Albert Powell Warrington, who had been a member of the Theosophical Society of Adyar since 1896. One resident of the Hollywood Krotona developed a science called stereometry, symbolized by a three-dimensional construction that took him fifteen years to build. This complex structure contained more than three tons of redwood sawed into over a million pieces and fitted into thousands of geometric forms in an attempt to illustrate the relation of spirit to matter and to prove the existence of the fourth dimension.

Krotona sold its 15 acres of fantastically valuable Hollywood real estate in 1924 and relocated on 118 acres in the Ojai Valley. The intention was "to establish and maintain an Ashrama that may be acceptable to the Great Ones; to make a training ground for the leaders now coming into incarnation, and to establish and maintain a school of Theosophy."[7]

Warrington was drawn to Ojai in part because the valley was once used as a "peace grounds" by the California Indians, and because great value was placed on the area's positive emanations, visible to some as a bright pyramid of light: "This Ojai Valley is an embodied Purpose, a splendid Jewel of the Future in a setting of to-day—both Jewel and setting miraculously merging into an Eternal beyond all shadows of time. . . . The Ojai Valley is the future laying hands upon the present, an End disclosing itself amidst the means, a Goal tangibly foreshadowed on the pathway leading to it."[8]

Warrington's widow still lives at Krotona, and she still believes the valley to be the birthplace of a new race, the sixth sub-race: "I can tell them just looking at them . . . long, thin, narrow hands, long, thin fingers. I can tell them the minute I see them, tell by their eyes. . . . Lemuria's beginning to come up again. That'll come up, and the sixth race will live on that."[9]

Today Krotona is basically a school of Theosophy. About forty members live on the grounds, only those who are needed to work in the library, to teach, and to maintain the magnificent formal gardens. There is a nominal charge for courses. The curriculum has included courses entitled Physics of the Spiritual World, The Human Aura, Nutrition and Vegetarian-

Annie Besant met Mme. Blavatsky and became a Theosophist shortly thereafter in 1889. Besant was a friend of Fabian socialists like George Bernard Shaw and of suffragettes like Susan B. Anthony. (Photo by Barraud, 1888; courtesy of the Huntington Library)

Annie Besant in Benares, India, in 1910, during one of her frequent visits to India. Following Mme. Blavatsky's death in 1891, Annie Besant became president of the large Theosophical faction whose headquarters were in Adyar, India. (Courtesy of Betty Warrington)

Alfred Powell Warrington in the early days of Theosophy. He later became general secretary of Krotona. (Courtesy of Betty Warrington)

ism, Mother Religions of the Races, and Occult Methods of Mental Development. There are restrictions on admittance to some of the courses, because some of the teachings cannot safely be given to the multitudes.

In 1971 the school was under the direction of Alfred Taylor, a retired professor of biology and biochemistry. He was old and bald and spare. He explained that the purpose of the school was not to teach the doctrines of Theosophy as such but to approach all fields of knowledge from a spiritual rather than a material point of view. Thus, guest professors at Krotona need not be members of the Theosophical Society so long as their vision is essentially spiritual. As proof that everything exists first in the mind, Taylor pointed to his desk as essentially an idea expressed through the materials used to construct it. He said that in his years of teaching biology he had never felt a contradiction between his roles as a scientist and as a Theosophist.

The goal of the school, as Taylor explained it, is to send good impulses out into the world to help all people to grow from within, without being subjected to external force. Only a few, however, are ready to receive these vibrations of gentleness and peace and

Warrington, a close friend of Annie Besant, founded the Krotona community in Hollywood in 1912 as the American Adyar, "a Sacred Center to which every occult mind will turn daily." This is the ceremonious laying of the cornerstone in Hollywood. (Courtesy of Betty Warrington)

The Krotona court under construction in the Hollywood hills in 1912. Although the automobile had made its debut by then, most drayage was still performed by horse and wagon. (Courtesy of Betty Warrington)

The court after completion in 1913. The once unpaved hills and streets in Hollywood are now covered with apartments and asphalt, and the court has been demolished. (Courtesy of Betty Warrington)

A close view of the court and temple. (Courtesy of Betty Warrington)

Office and publication work at Krotona, ca. 1913. (Courtesy of Betty Warrington)

"Krotona Lotus Group—1913." (Courtesy of Betty Warrington)

C. W. Leadbeater was one of Annie Besant's close associates. Although he was plagued by scandals that forced his resignation from the Theosophists, he remained close to Krotona. Leadbeater was a prolific writer in the Theosophical movement. One striking book that he coauthored with Annie Besant was *Thought Forms*. (Courtesy of Betty Warrington)

brotherhood. Those who cannot be reached yet, those who cling to violent ways, will be different a few lives from now; they are simply young souls. "In a future world-period, many millions of years off, progressive conditions will necessarily be such that only those who have attained to human perfection will go on into the still higher reaches of evolution, and these very distinctly will be the saved ones, as a group, in the sense of being the garnered fruitage of the present evolution."[10]

Taylor dismissed Point Loma by saying that Katherine Tingley was a medium and that true Theosophy was opposed to mediumship. He declared "messing around with occult powers" to be contrary to his beliefs. Magic, he said, leads to death and ruin. (Mrs. Tingley actually disavowed "psychism," however, whereas Annie Besant, revered by the Krotona Theosophists, never stopped making prophecies, although she often regretted them later. Krotona's official repudiation of occultism, therefore, apparently reflects a change of policy since the old days.)

Krotona has just a few young members. They acknowledge that the society is dying, that almost everyone is old, and that the group does not really do anything anymore, but they value what Theosophy has to teach. Annie Besant once wrote:

We believe . . . that this Society was not formed by the ordinary impulse that draws men together who are interested in a common society, but that it was designed, conceived and started by some of the superhuman Men who

"Inside library—Krotona L.A. ca. 1912." (Courtesy of Betty Warrington)

Annie Besant brought J. Krishnamurti into the Theo-sophical movement when he was only fourteen. At the time of this photograph, 1912, he was in England, study-ing at Oxford. *The American Theosophist* said at that time: "Alcyone [Krishnamurti's pen name] is the head of a world-wide organization known as the Order of the Star in the East, whose chief purpose is to herald the near coming of the World Teacher, Who is expected to solve the great problems of the day."

The Ternary Building, which faced the court and the stadium, ca. 1914. It is now an apartment building and looks very much the same, but the pond is gone. (Cour-tesy of Betty Warrington)

are the Spiritual Guardians of the human race, and who employed one of their own disciples, H. P. Blavatsky, to bring about its formation. . . . May no member who reads this article ever be so blinded by ignorance as to throw away the priceless privilege he has won and so lose his share of the glorious function of being a life-bringer to the world![11]

V. THE OJAI VALLEY

Annie Besant once declared the Ojai Valley (home of Edgar Holloway, who claimed to have come from Mu on a flying fish) to be the magnetic center of the earth. Krotona moved to the Ojai Valley in 1924, and about 1925 an additional 150 acres in the upper Ojai Valley was purchased for the Order of the Star in the East for the purpose of a camp and possibly a school. The Order of the Star in the East was founded by Annie Besant for J. Krishnamurti, an Indian she pro-claimed to be the new world teacher.

Krishnamurti was born in Madras in 1895. His father was a Theosophist who worked at the society's headquarters at Adyar. In 1909 Mrs. Besant rec-ognized latent faculties in Krishnamurti that she be-lieved would make him a great spiritual teacher. She offered to give him the education necessary for his mission, and his father accepted. In 1911, when Krishnamurti was sixteen, she took him to Europe

After his stay in England, Krishnamurti came to the United States in 1922 and stayed in Ojai. (Courtesy of Betty Warrington)

and publicly announced the nature of his spiritual greatness. Thousands of Theosophists accepted her proclamation and formed the Order of the Star in the East to prepare the way for Krishnamurti's work.

Mrs. Besant came to Ojai for a visit in October, 1926, when plans were discussed for the building of the proposed camp in the upper valley. It was discovered, however, that the site was unsuitable because of the lack of water, and it was decided to establish the Star Camp on acreage near Krotona Hill. Annie Besant then bought the 150 acres from the Order of the Star in the East for a project that came to be known as the Happy Valley community scheme. She planned to build a world religious center on the land, with Krishnamurti as its head.

In 1929 Krishnamurti denied the claims made for him, dissolved the Order of the Star, and disassociated himself from the Theosophical Society, holding that an organization dedicated to spiritual purposes must by its nature become a barrier to the individual's search. Although the Theosophical Society was certainly embarrassed by his move, Annie Besant never relinquished her belief in Krishnamurti. Years later she said publicly, "Either he is the world teacher, or I am a liar."

Krishnamurti has now spent more that forty years traveling, lecturing, and attempting to prevent organizations from springing up around him. Perhaps there will be a religion in his name after his death, but in his long life he has consistently rejected the idea of religious authority: "If I say that I am the Christ, you will create another authority. If I say I am not, you will also create another authority. Do you think that Truth has anything to do with what you think I am? . . . If I say to you that I am, and another says to you that I am not the Christ—where will you be? Put aside the label, for that has no value."[12]

Mrs. Besant's vision of a religious center in Ojai was of course never realized, but Krishnamurti did make his home in Ojai for a number of years. In 1946 Krishnamurti, Aldous Huxley, and others founded a secondary school in Ojai, called Happy Valley. The school is completely nonsectarian. It does not teach the ideas of Theosophy or the ideas of Krishnamurti: "We try to foster in each student the spirit of inquiry and at all times to avoid the arbitrary imposition of ideas. It is directly contrary to our policy to practice any kind of political or religious indoctrination." The motto of the school is *Aun Apprendo,* and it means "I am still learning."

Happy Valley School bought the land originally planned by Mrs. Besant as the religious center of the sixth world race. Several of the school's present direc-

Krotona moved from Los Angeles to Ojai in 1924. Krishnamurti spoke with young students at his Order of the Star in the East Camp in 1928.

tors knew Mrs. Besant and Krishnamurti for many years. So the school is, in a sense, an outgrowth of the Theosophical movement, and one that is very much alive. Happy Valley has lavish plans for expansion, and a few lines from the architects' report to the school gives an indication of its direction: "The arrangement of stringing buildings like a crown around the brow of each hill not only does no violence to the hill (no bulldozers flattening our hilltops; no mediocrity levelling our spirits) but also creates a hillcrest 'commons' garden for each school. Commons should not only imply community but should actually create it."

      ✢   ✢   ✢

At the turn of this century, as disillusionment was growing with the fixed and dogmatic teachings of established religion, some thinkers proposed a return

The Star Camp in Ojai was several miles from the Krotona grounds and was communally organized. (Courtesy of Betty Warrington)

"1928—Our Messenger Corps at Star Camp. Ojai, California." (Courtesy of Betty Warrington)

The kitchen of the 1928 Star Camp. The structure later became the Happy Valley School Administration Building. (Courtesy of Betty Warrington)

to the traditional sacred writings—the Old and New Testaments, the Vedas, and so forth. There was an attempt to get behind the meaning of the scriptures, rather than taking the writings in a literal, or wholly external, way. Several groups were formed to explore the mysterious nature of the traditional sacred writings. Among these groups were the Theosophists.

Feeling there was a richer life hidden in the traditional teachings, the Theosophists tried to plumb deeper and to evoke a genuinely religious life in their communities. The Theosophical communities began to grow increasingly rigid in their thinking, however; the members built new edifices and espoused new philosophies that they took as the final word. They began to worship their own institutions, as even now some former members of Point Loma and Krotona live in the memories of their communities' accomplishments. As the forms of their institutions became increasingly more important, and as the sense of mystery that first interested the Theosophists lessened, any knowledge they might have gathered disappeared. The commune became a church in itself, and knowledge—which is not rigid—was forgotten in the forms. In this way Theosophy became old and decrepit: The fixed forms and achievements of an earlier day lost whatever inner meaning they may have had, and young members were not attracted to what had become stale. It is interesting that the "heretics" from Point Loma—those who studied at the community and then went their own way to teach what they had learned (and are now blacklisted by the rigid old guard)—

The Administration Building at Happy Valley School was
scheduled for demolition in 1971, at the time this photograph was made. (Photograph by Paul Kagan)

On August 3, 1929, Krishnamurti gave a speech at a Star Camp convention in Ommen, Holland, in which he denied the claims made for him, dissolved the Order of the Star, and disassociated himself from the Theosophical Society.

The library (left) at Krotona, Ojai (pictured in the 1930's), still functions, with Betty Robertson Warrington (above) as its present-day librarian. Her 1915 diploma (below) was signed by A. P. Warrington. Later, they became man and wife. (Courtesy of Betty Warrington; photograph of Betty Warrington by Paul Kagan)

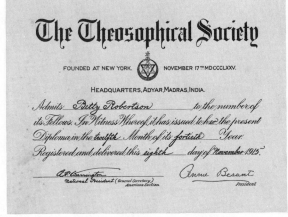

are the ones who have most successfully used the richness of their education at Point Loma. They teach in places like the East-West Cultural Center in Los Angeles, or they bring their learning to new communal experiments.

It should be remembered that discipline was imposed at Point Loma to the extent of totally separating a child from the outside world. No newspapers or telephones prepared the child's thinking for the mundane realities of a chaotic society. If there are benefits from a communal education, are they at the expense of blinding the communards to worldly problems?

Do the alumni of a commune leave unable to face the realities of city life? If any conclusion can be drawn from these questions, it is that any externally imposed discipline is dangerous. If some freedom is not left for children to search for their own education, the "little lotus-buds" of Point Loma can grow into rigid, narrow moralists and disciplinarians or into sparkle-eyed dreamers of great things past.

This astrological sundial now graces the spacious lawns of the Krotona community at Ojai. Once it stood near the Ternary Building at the original Krotona location in Hollywood. (Photograph by Paul Kagan)

Among the organizers of Happy Valley School in 1946 were (left to right) D. Rajagopal, Krishnamurti, Maria Huxley, and Aldous Huxley. (Courtesy of Rosalind Rajagopal)

Happy Valley School is expanding and building new quarters today in the Ojai Valley, under the able direction of Rosalind Rajagopal. The girls' dormitory on the "upper campus" of Happy Valley is the first building of a proposed educational community. Happy Valley School is one outgrowth of the seeds planted by Annie Besant. (Photographs by Paul Kagan)

The Kaweah colonists assembled around the Karl Marx tree in the late 1880's. This California Sequoia tree was later renamed the General Sherman tree after the colonists were forced out by the government. (Courtesy of the Bancroft Library)

CHAPTER 5

Kaweah Co-operative Commonwealth

The Kaweah Co-operative Commonwealth was born in the high mountains of the Sierras, partly in what is now Sequoia National Park. When Kaweah was begun in the 1880's, the hopes of the founders were to create a kind of Christian anarchy, a mixture of Marxism and utopian socialism. Money was absent from Kaweah; the medium of exchange was a certificate of labor hours.

The greatest material asset of the colony, its timber holdings, proved the point of dispute over which the commune failed. The U.S. government, anxious to crush the seeds of an early "red menace" and to protect huge private California timber interests, managed to evict the colonists from their encampment-cities in order to found Sequoia Park in September, 1890, presumably in the interests of ecology. The government was not primarily concerned with the preservation of the land, however, but with the destruction of a socialist experiment. Kaweah's Karl Marx tree was renamed the General Sherman tree. It is ironic that the site of Kaweah is commemorated with a metal plaque, one of the few instances in which the government has officially recognized a utopian scheme.

"We meant to create amid the hills an ideal commonwealth, the Fraternal Republic of which the world will always dream." Burnette G. Haskell, a brilliant but erratic West Coast labor leader and cofounder of the Kaweah Co-operative Commonwealth, included these words in his epitaph for Kaweah, published in the San Francisco *Examiner* on November 29, 1891.

Haskell was born in Sierra County, California, in 1857. He attended school in California and the Midwest and in 1879 was admitted to the California bar. He soon took a dislike to the law, however, and became editor of a labor journal. In 1885 Haskell, with fellow labor leader James J. Martin, headed a group filing claims on timber land near Visalia, California, with the intention of forming a colony. Kaweah's "deed of settlement" stated its aims: "To improve the health, secure the happiness and perfect the well being of each and every member. And as well to propagate and extend in the world at large the idea of universal and just cooperation." The inspiration for the colony was Laurence Gronlund's *Co-operative Commonwealth,* a book that attempted to translate Marx into practical American terms. Gronlund's suggested basic organizational structure for a colony was accepted with some alterations by Kaweah.

Haskell and Martin were very much aware of any colony's need for economic self-sufficiency. In the midst of their search for a product that would assure a steady income, word came from an associate of Haskell's of the magnificent redwood forests near Visalia. Timber was highly marketable, and the prospective colonists thought the economic foundation of Kaweah would be securely established as soon as their claims on the land were filed. However, in the very act of filing their claims, the seeds of Kaweah's destruction were planted. Because of previous timber frauds farther north, the land agents were suspicious of so many claims filed at one time. Kaweah's claims came under the jurisdiction of federal law—the Timberland Act of 1878 and the Homestead Act of 1862 —and the Visalia land agents communicated their suspicions of fraud to Washington. Two months after the claims were filed, they were officially under investigation by the federal government. The colonists failed to realize the serious implications of not having clear title to the land and were confident that everything would be decided in their favor, since they were convinced that they had committed no fraud.

Even before the storm of protest broke over the colony's plans to log the ancient forests, Kaweah was having trouble generated by its own bureaucracy. The colony was established with three major divisions, thirteen departments, more than fifty bureaus, and innumerable sections. This cumbersome hierarchical government was eventually reduced to eight departments, under a board of trustees, and a general meeting, which was the court of last appeal. Haskell, in his *Examiner* article of 1891, gives us this description:

This General Meeting, which assembled monthly, assumed, like the Athenian popular assemblies, to deal with details, and it made confusion worse confounded. Members drew pay while attending it, and at one time it lasted four days at a stretch. Generally what one month's meeting ordered the next would rescind. Under its domination we suffered from all the evils of popular assemblages such as we read of in the books. We had not believed what we read; now we knew they did not tell the half of it. . . . I have seen a woman getting in firewood with an ax and bucksaw in plain sight of thirteen men gathered for six solid hours around a stump excitedly discussing a rule of order improperly construed at the last meeting.

Kaweah was simply unable to translate its dazzling vision into the practical terms of cooperative production. Its main task at its inception was to build a road into what had been considered inaccessible forests. The trees could not be felled and the logs transported without the road. For most of its short life Kaweah drained its energy into the road, a symbol for the power of cooperative labor. In Haskell's own words:

This stupendous work, for such it was, was begun October 8, 1886. . . . It was finished, entering the pines in June, 1890, nearly four years later. It is eighteen miles long, winding around hill and through canyon to attain the elevation, 8,000 feet, on a steady, noble grade of eight feet to the hundred, although on an air line the distance

Burnette G. Haskell, cofounder of the Kaweah Co-operative Commonwealth, had been a lawyer and West Coast labor leader before his communal experiment in "Christian anarchy." (Courtesy of the Bancroft Library)

An application for membership to Kaweah that arrived too late; the colony's demise came before John McDonough could join. (Courtesy of the Bancroft Library)

C. C. Curtis made many of the fine photographs of Kaweah. This is an early survey party on Haskell's Bluff in 1884 or 1885. (Courtesy of the Bancroft Library)

The road-building at Kaweah took place from 1886 to 1890. Eighteen miles long, this monument to communal endeavor is still in use as a fire road in Sequoia National Park. (Engraving from the San Francisco *Examiner*, November 29, 1891, courtesy of the Bancroft Library)

This is the "Advance Guard," a group of road-builders, and the tent city of Advance they occupied in September of 1889. (Courtesy of the Bancroft Library)

Currency at Kaweah was based on an exact value of labor time.
This is a 200-minute bill. (Courtesy of the Bancroft Library)

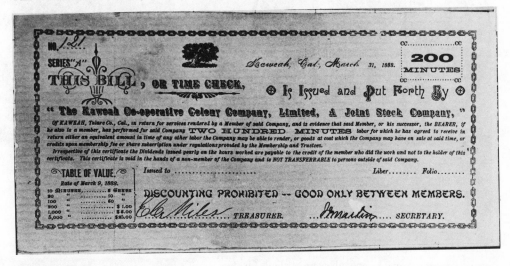

to be gained does not exceed three miles. An average of twenty men worked at the task continuously until done, and without proper tools, powder or other appliances.

The road is Kaweah's monument and can be traveled today.

Once the timber was reached, however, the logging was never carried out efficiently. Haskell acknowledged in 1891 that

the actual cut averaged . . . less than a tenth of what ought to be done, and this mill was not run short-handed. It is true that most of the time it did not run; that the loggers were inexpert; that the mill was small and old; that picnics had to be organized; that the men had to come down for "general meeting"; that this foreman was bad and that foreman was worse; that the timber was small; that the oxen were lame, and a hundred other reasons; but the fact remains that results were not attained as they are in the competitive world.

This admission must have come hard only two years after the young colony published *A Pen Picture of Kaweah* in 1889:

Here all shall receive the full value of their labor and each shall labor for the good of all. Here the Man shall

be sunk in the State and yet shall be given such freedom for growth and development that he, like some golden pinnacle of a perfect palace, shall tower far above the foundation walls. . . . Here shall be Joy, Music and Laughter, Art, Science and Beauty and all things else for which Poets have sung and Martyrs died, and of which in the outer world we see but the palest phantoms.

Kaweah did make every effort to look after the intellectual and recreational interests of its members as well as their political needs. The colony was born with the belief that economic security would come so easily that there would be plenty of time to pursue artistic and cultural projects. A temple and theater were planned, to be built of marble. An active attempt was made to attract members with intellectual interests. Application blanks at one time required prospective members to list the books on economics, politics, and history that they had recently read, and the membership (which at its peak numbered around three hundred) certainly embraced a wide range of interests. Haskell mentions

temperance men and their opposite, churchmen and agnostics, free-thinkers, Darwinists and spiritualists, bad poets and good, musicians, artists, prophets and priests. There

Another piece of Kaweah currency: a 24-hour coin. (Courtesy of the Bancroft Library)

were dress-reform cranks and phonetic spelling fanatics, word-purists and vegetarians. It was a mad, mad world, and being so small its madness was the more visible.

Perhaps all they shared was an interest in the social and economic questions of their day, and perhaps that was not enough. At any rate, most of Kaweah's cultural projects somehow went awry. Haskell enumerated a few in 1891:

Various attempts were made to organize a band and an orchestra, but the membership changed so often that nothing permanent resulted. . . . Literary and scientific classes were started but petered out from lack of interest. . . . A series of "Mothers' meetings" broke up through bickerings and want of something definite to do.
Dances were occasionally had, though they met with strenuous opposition from a few who believed dancing a sin.
Instead of the fraternal, friendly feeling hoped for, one found Kaweah divided into factions, and fractions of factions. Discussions about what Brown had to eat, and

A temporary bridge built by the early colonists across the north fork of the Kaweah River. It was washed away by a flood within a year after its construction. (Courtesy of the Bancroft Library)

"The colony tractor taking a bath." It had fallen through a bridge. (Courtesy of the Bancroft Library)

"The Camp of the Colonists at the Atwell Mill. This Mill was leased by the Colonists·pending the decision in relation to their timber claims from which they had been driven by the Military. Here, too, the Military attempted to drive them away but were stopped by state injunction." (Courtesy of the Bancroft Library)

how Smith was pretending to be sick to escape work were met with, instead of an interest in literature and art. . . .

Another hope of the colonists was that of educational facilities. . . . But removed from the restraints of the competitive world parents and children alike were unable to distinguish between liberty and license. . . . The teachers found it impossible to enforce discipline when a child who deemed himself aggrieved would in the class openly threaten that he would go home and get his father to call a meeting and remove the instructor.

Even if Kaweah had survived the internal quarrels, it still might have gone under as a result of external pressures that had nothing to do with its problems with the U.S. government. The San Francisco papers consistently attacked the colony. In December, 1889, the *Chronicle* published an article under the headline "Lawyer Haskell's Game. His Followers Claim That They Have Been Duped and Swindled." By 1890 the paper went so far as to speak of "delicate women, tender children, obliged to brave the storms of winter in canvas houses, fed on beans and bacon coarsely cooked, forced to perform the most menial labor." The same year witnessed a quarrel over seventy-two dollars allegedly owed to a colonist by Haskell. The colonist, James Kennedy, went to court for his money, and the San Francisco *Report* (December 27) sneeringly headlined its story "The Beauties of Bellamyism Developing at Kaweah." (Although Kaweah was founded before *Looking Backward* was published and the Nationalist movement begun, the colony was often associated with Nationalism.)

More important, around this time articles began to appear under headlines such as "Saving the Sequoias. A Protest Against More Vandalism" (*Chronicle*, November 20, 1890) and "The Big Trees. A Noble Forest in Danger From Settlers" (*Report*, December 27, 1890). In early January, 1891, the trustees of Kaweah were formally charged with cutting timber on government land. Although the public boundary had been unintentionally crossed and only five pines had been felled, the trustees were declared guilty and fined $301 apiece (they were later pardoned by President William McKinley). The San Francisco *Call* (April 7, 1891) ran the headline "A Bursted Bubble. Probable End of the Kaweah Colony Scheme. The Trustees Convicted of Cutting Timber on Government Land. How the Bellamyites Were Duped by Cunning Men—Time and Money of the Victims Lost." The Los Angeles *Evening Express* (April 16, 1891) published an exposé, "a shameful revelation of theft, delusion, cruelty and oppression, whereby the government was sought to be robbed and numbers of ignorant and confiding people swin-

"Wolverton's cabin—hollowed out of a log." (Courtesy of the Bancroft Library and *Out West*)

dled." The reporter was not only concerned with the timber case but also managed to find a one-time colony member who felt cheated by conditions at Kaweah: "There has been just enough rice, sugar, fruit and tapioca to say we had them; and if our buyers have one talent above another it is in buying the cheapest and meanest provisions in the market."

After the 1891 court decision there were no new legal moves to oust the colonists until early the following year, but the vindictive press continued to make things uncomfortable. Much was made over Levi "Father" Elphick, an old "newsboy" of eccentric habits from San Francisco who died at Kaweah. The *Chronicle* reported his death with a long story on

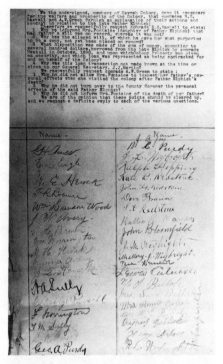

The untimely death of Father Elphick resulted in uncomfortable rumors. Kaweah was vindicated, but only after further damage to the colony's reputation by newspapers. (Courtesy of the Bancroft Library)

July 28, 1891; their dispatch from Kaweah said that Elphick had joined the colony as a nonresident the year before, had arrived a few days before his death, and had died of heat prostration after picking beans. On July 31 the *Chronicle* published another story with the headline "Elphick's Death. Rumors of Foul Play Freely Circulated. He Went to Look After His Kaweah Investment and Was Found Dead." The article stated that the frugal old man had gone to Kaweah to see about recovering eight hundred dollars he had allegedly loaned the colony and had died mysteriously. As support for its story the *Chronicle* cited an ex-member's claim that at Kaweah "those who displease the managers are slowly starved to death." Even members of the colony were disturbed by the rumors, and many signed a petition to Haskell requesting that certain questions be cleared up, including what happened to Elphick's money.

The San Francisco *Examiner* of August 1 published Elphick's will, which left everything to his daughter, and the paper mentioned rumors that the old man had been poisoned but righteously declared them unfounded because of Kaweah's generally law-abiding character. This story was followed on August 14 by

One of Kaweah's pastoral moments—communal bathing in an unspoiled setting. (Courtesy of the Bancroft Library)

an emphatic statement that Elphick was most certainly not murdered. The *Examiner* claimed to have made its own investigation of the case and concluded that "Elphick had been stricken fatally with apoplexy while preparing to take a bath, and that the stories of foul play had no foundation whatever." Kaweah was vindicated, but only after newspaper innuendo had inflicted further damage to its reputation.

It is worthy of note that through all the assaults from the big-city papers, the local press supported Kaweah. The Tulare County *Times*, for example, ran a long article (August 20, 1891) commending Kaweah as "a prosperous and harmonious colony, putting the co-operative theory in operation" and accomplishing great works in spite of "unwarranted persecution by the government." When the *Chronicle* (September 22, 1891) claimed that the Haskell-Martin partnership had thrived "at the expense of all honest men and women who have come within the reach of their clutches," the *Times* rushed to their defense (September 24), calling the attack "brutal" and "libelous." Several months later, when a weary Kaweah was limping toward its dissolution, the *Times* mourned in advance (November 11), saying that "the whole machinery of the government was being set in motion [in creating Sequoia National Park on the land claimed by Kaweah] to starve out a body of industrious, inoffensive and intelligent people." When federal troops

"Three Hopping Kiddies, Claire, Dorothy and George." (Courtesy of the Bancroft Library)

Sierra winters meant snow—and snowball fights at Kaweah (ca. 1889). (Courtesy of the Bancroft Library)

"A rather rough looking picture of one of our tents with the contents outside." The same tent is in the background of the snowball fight. (Courtesy of the Bancroft Library)

Kaweah, October 6, 1891.

Dear Dad and Benjie:

Haskell Family Collection
Bancroft Library

The enclosed explain themselves and show what the situation is down here. The statement about tmhe Green affair went down to the District Attorney to day; meanwhile I am out of money and soon will be out of grub; I wish you could send me in registered letter $5 or $10 , and could also buy for me and ship the following by freight, prepaid.

I know how hard up you are but I hope you can get this for me; I will try and return it before very long.

Send packed in a box addressed to   Chas. Hoyt, Kaweah, Colony, via Visalia, Cal. the following:

Granulated sugar...$1.00
Rolled oats or oatmeal......................................1.00
One can of lard...50
White beans...25   .25
Salt pork...25
Bacon or ham 1.00

With this I can get through another month if necessary.

If you can't get it why then let it rip but let me know and I will do my best to rustle it up around here. The Barnard, Martin outfit are trying to starve me out; they will not even bring up things for me on the stage when I buy them in Visalia.

They will also try and starve out all who signed the treasurers circular, enclosed. More anon. All well. Yours,

Brunette G Haskell

Times got harder, and Haskell was arrested. (Courtesy of the Bancroft Library)

This letter from Haskell evidenced the hard times befalling Kaweah. (Courtesy of the Bancroft Library)

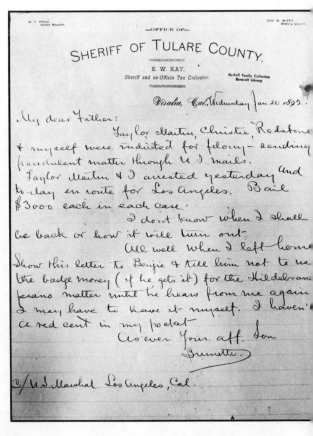

W. P. GRILL,
Under Sheriff.   GEO W. WITT,
                                                      Deputy Sheriff.

—OFFICE OF—

SHERIFF OF TULARE COUNTY.

E. W. KAY,
Sheriff and ex-Officio Tax Collector.

Haskell Family Collection
Bancroft Library

Visalia, Cal, Wednesday Jan 20 1892.

My dear Father:

Taylor Martin, Christie Redstone & myself were indicted for felony — sending fraudulent matter through U.S. mails.

Taylor Martin & I arrested yesterday and to-day en route for Los Angeles. Bail $3000 each in each case.

I don't know when I shall be back or how it will turn out.

All well when I left home. Show this letter to Benjie & tell him not to use the badge money (if he gets it) for the Hildebrand piano matter until he hears from me again. I may have to have it myself. I haven't a red cent in my pocket.

As ever Your aff. Son

Brunette

c/ U.S. Marshal Los Angeles, Cal.

Haskell's cabin, and a note he posted on the door to protect his belongings. Kaweah was no longer a common enterprise, and all property matters were confused. (Courtesy of the Bancroft Library)

were sent in to administer the new park in 1890, the local press had labeled it "Cossack terrorism," and residents of the nearby towns had booed the soldiers in the streets and shot at them in the forests.

During the decline of Kaweah a young man from Colorado who wished to come to the colony with his bride became so despondent that he shot himself. The press attributed the suicide to the failure of cooperation, and Haskell was further embittered. He clearly foresaw the death of his vision, at least as it existed at Kaweah. He wrote to his mother as early as October 28, 1891, of his plans to homestead on a piece of Kaweah land "as soon as the colony busts." In fact, several colonists hoped to turn the land into independent cooperative farms, but no agreement was reached on the division of the property, and the plan was abandoned.

The end of Kaweah as a colony came in January, 1892, when the trustees were indicted for using the mail to defraud by sending out colony propaganda and soliciting donations. Haskell wrote to his father on stationery headed "Office of Sheriff of Tulare County," saying that his bail was three thousand dollars and that "I haven't a red cent in my pocket." He was finally released after his bail was reduced to five hundred dollars when he pleaded "abject poverty." When the case came to trial, the jury acquitted on the basis of insufficient evidence, but Kaweah's short history was ended. Haskell had spent the month between his arrest and the trial at Kaweah watching the remaining families pack up, often quarreling over the disposition of community belongings. He blamed nothing so much as human nature, arguing that "men are not yet civilized enough to do right for right's sake alone and to labor for the love of production itself."

In 1902 Haskell revised his *Examiner* article, and it was published in *Out West*. "We were not fit to survive and we died," he wrote. "But there is no bribe money in our pockets; and beaten and ragged as we are, we are not ashamed. . . . And is there no remedy, then, for the evils that oppress the poor? And is there no surety that the day is coming when justice and right shall reign on earth? I do not know; but I believe, and I hope, and I trust."[1] Haskell died in November, 1907, poor and friendless.

The Kaweah post office, built several years after the colony's demise, is still in use. It can be viewed on the way into the Sierra wilderness. (Photograph by Paul Kagan)

William Riker ran for governor of California several times. This is a campaign leaflet that issued from the Holy City Press in the 1940's. (Courtesy of the Bancroft Library)

CALIFORNIA
IS A White Man's Home
═══ AND ═══
WILLIAM E. RIKER
Your Next Governor Says:

"Orientals prepare to accept a job and get out of our white race man's business, as we do not need your help in any way."

The White Man can take care of any and all kinds of business in our own, White Man's California State Home, and no longer will the White Man tolerate their undermining and polluting tactics. Farmers, Business Men and the Workers say: Orientals get out and stay out of our business. Our new Government will see that you get a job. Their polluting, undermining system of business must eternally stop in Our White Man's Home and besides this, they must keep their polluting hands off our White Race Women; they belong only to us White Race People. This is the true law of our Original White Man's CONSTITUTION, and it explains the real and true spirit of California.

TAKE NOTICE

William E. RIKER'S Perfect Platform, Perfect Labor Solution, Perfect Message, Perfect System of Government, and His PERFECT ABUSE, AND GRAFT PROOF PENSION PLAN, IS NOW HEREIN EXPLAINED AND READY FOR EVERYONE to UNDERSTAND AND VOTE FOR.

CHAPTER 6

Holy City

In heart and mind—in purpose,
*   On this rock that's firm and dry*
They are building a New City
*   For the Godlike and Most High,*
Where they'll dwell in peace and comfort,
*   From the serpents face away;*
This cult, so-called, now landed,
*   Is the Perfect Christian Way.*
                    —Mother Lucille Riker

Holy City epitomizes the bizarre aspect of nontraditional, ephemeral communes. In every way it supports the stereotype of cultic fanatics in the land of the lotus-eaters. It lasted from 1919 until the late 1950's in the Santa Cruz Mountains of central California. Alcoholic soda pop, peep shows of naked ladies, special holy spring water, and an ornately decorated gas station were part of the attractions that lured passing motorists to spend their money in William E. Riker's colony. When the tourists stopped, they could not miss the screaming messages of the "World's Perfect Government," a religious-political mishmash of Riker's slogans, based on racism and hate. The privileged position Riker accorded to whites built the psychological wall against the outside world that unified the members of his colony.

William E. Riker, founder of the Perfect Christian Divine Way (P.C.D.W.), first became news in 1909, when he threatened to kidnap his infant child from a woman who had just discovered their union to be bigamous. Newspaper accounts reported that Riker, then thirty-six years old, fled north from Oakland, California, disguised behind a heavy false beard, when the new mother, Mrs. Bessie Riker, learned of the existence of Mrs. Marene Riker. One paper pointed out that Riker, in his role as a healer, placed special emphasis on his ability to explain love and solve problems between husbands and wives.

Neither woman filed bigamy charges, and the incident rapidly passed out of the public interest, but it reflects the tone of Riker's panoramic yet pathetic career as man of God, politician, philosopher, cult leader, and showman. The press was drawn to him, because there was always a story; the public was drawn to him, because he knew how to entertain. Although many found his ideas or his style outrageous or repulsive, he was almost never dull.

In 1919 Riker and his new wife, Lucille, moved the P.C.D.W., with about thirty followers, from its headquarters on Hayes Street in San Francisco to his own version of the New Jerusalem. Holy City, California, was founded on a few acres in the Santa Cruz Mountains, between Santa Cruz and San Jose. The land, which eventually included almost two hundred acres, was bordered by a state highway, but it was still green and quiet. Within a few years the colonists numbered in the hundreds; they had built cabins, a

These crumbling concrete steps lead to the house that was once William E.
Riker's. Riker was the founder and despotic ruler of the Holy City community for over forty years. (Photograph by Paul Kagan)

Father Riker, photographed in 1938. (Courtesy of the Los Angeles *Times*)

Mother Lucille was William Riker's cohort throughout the heyday and eventual decline of Holy City. (Courtesy of the Bancroft Library)

Two Women Claim "Healer" as Husband

OAKLAND, Jan. 5. — Deserted by her husband, Edwin Riker, who styles himself a divine healer and is the founder of a new religious cult, Mrs. Bessie Zetta Riker is living in Oakland with her 4 months old son, grief stricken by the discovery that the man she married is, according to her information, a bigamist. Riker has fled from the city and it is believed that he is now in British Columbia. His first wife, Mrs. Marcus Riker, who apprised her youthful successor that she had been a victim of criminal deceit, is living at the Globe hotel, Thirteenth street and Broadway, in this city.

Riker deserted his second wife three days after the birth of her child when he learned that she knew of his alleged duplicity. After his departure Mrs. Riker says her husband wrote to her saying that he intended to take possession of his child, and that he would resort to any measures to carry out his desire. This threat has been repeated and, fearing that it would be carried out, Mrs. Riker has applied to the police for protection against the vanished healer.

Captain of Detectives Petersen informed her that the law required her to go to Pasadena, where her marriage to Riker was performed, if she desired to swear to a bigamy complaint against him. As the expense of the trip was so great Mrs. Riker decided to dispense with the complaint, but she has lived in continual fear that Riker would try to steal her baby.

The discovery that Riker was already married was made three days after the birth of Mrs. Riker's child, while the mother was still confined to her bed. Mrs. Riker No. 1 heard of the child's birth and visited the hotel where the "divine healer" was living with his second wife. Going to the door of the young mother's room she demanded an interview with Riker. He went out into the hall and attempted to pacify her, but Mrs. Riker the first was extremely threatening in her demeanor, it is said, and is alleged to have demanded money as the price of silence. The second wife's sister overheard the conversation, and informed Mrs. Riker No. 2 of the circumstances.

Riker left the city at once and no definite news of him has been received since, save in the threatening letters which he sent to the young mother.

Riker formerly rented a room in a building in Thirteenth street, where he lectured several times a week, and secured a number of converts to his teachings. He advertised himself as a wonder worker and healer, and dwelt with particular emphasis upon his ability to explain the mysteries of love and to unravel matrimonial tangles.

Mrs. Bessie Riker, wife No. 2, and Edwin Riker, the alleged bigamist.

Even before the founding of Holy City, the San Francisco *Chronicle* was obtaining good mileage from Riker's exploits in 1909. (Courtesy of the San Francisco *Chronicle*)

Man can run away from his enemies by becoming a bigger one.
Keep out of the Devil's way by living in his ways innocently.

The Enlightener
HAS COME TO ETERNALLY STAND BY YOU
EDITED BY THE P.C.D.W. —— SAN FRANCISCO, CAL.

VOL. 3   SAN FRANCISCO, CAL.   DECEMBER 15, 1918   No. 8

¶ MORTAL MAN EATS THE SWEETS OF THE EARTH AND THE POISON OF WOMAN; THE WISE MAN DOES THE OPPOSITE.

THE POISON OF THE EARTH

The poison of earth is strong medicine and all mortal women who typify mother earth are well loaded with it, for the purpose of either curing or destroying man and it is ever being transmitted to him from her through space mentally. Other diseases that he contracts from her through being in physical contact are only a warning and gentle hint of this more deadly poison. The way to escape it is to develop strength sufficient to convert her into being your own flesh and blood.

GRANDEUR

A grown person sees the grandeur of child life, not because it is grand which in truth it is not compared with their own matured life, but because he or she is in the grand matured position and this makes them see the grandeur of child life.

Keep in tune with the spirit of the movement you behold, or you may be pushed aside; willing to obey its command is the way.

THE DEVIL'S KINGDOM

The Solar System is the Devil's Kingdom, from which we must be born as a child from its mother's womb. Negative thoughts and people are a Devil to the flesh as mortal woman is to man after he is created, and the wise man is to his enemies. After coming into the final light it is then we see clearly that the Devil his, ways and kingdom is a God to be worshiped in order to qualify us to worship the final impersonal God.

P. C. D. W. DIAMONDS

Diamonds of the earth makes the physical body appear beautiful, but diamonds of the P.C.D.W. Wisdom make the body itself beautiful. He who possesses such Diamonds can charm anyone though he wears ragged and dirty clothes.

The greatest light is the laws of life, and he who discovers and lives them, it is he who is a light.

DIVINE DESTRUCTION

Having your mind centered on divine destruction instead of construction indicates your maturity, and gives the Divine Law a chance to create for you a pure atmosphere to live in. What mortal man creates outside of himself is his stumblingblock, but what the Divine law creates is his freedom.

Whenever you are able to connect construction and destruction and intermingle them to the degree you discern no division or separation, you are vibrating in mastery.

Fool not yourself with your fake purity as long as there is impurity in the world.

Discover Wisdom impurity and then you are pure, until the final purity comes into the world.

Give up your game, your name, your life to the Master mind, in order to live, instead of giving it up to darkness the day of your death.

Riker expounded the "Perfect Christian Divine Way" (P.C.D.W.) from his Hayes Street headquarters in San Francisco in 1918, just months before the move to Holy City in the Santa Cruz mountains. (Courtesy of the Bancroft Library)

service station, a grocery store, a restaurant, a bakery, a shoe repair shop, a barber shop, and a printing office and were thriving on the tourist trade provided by the conveniently situated highway. Riker, always effective at attracting attention, covered the walls of Holy City with paintings and signs: "Father Riker, the king of all wise men, gives to the world a new and perfect form of government. $25,000 reward if you can find any flaws in it. We ask your investigation. My new system guarantees heaven on this earth." Riker set up a row of wooden Santa Clauses on the main street, each with an axiom printed on its stomach: "When woman says no she means yes in the end and when man says yes he means no in the end. Figure this out if you can." In Holy City's heyday, throughout the twenties and thirties, business expanded to include a factory producing ginger ale and Golden Glow beer (reportedly sold under the counter during Prohibition), peep shows with a religious theme, a mystery hall, an observatory, and a zoo.

In 1921 Riker was charged by a county grand jury with conspiracy to commit acts injurious to public morals, conspiracy to obtain money by false promises, grand larceny, and embezzlement. The district attorney announced to the press that the case was "outrageous . . . from a standpoint of immorality and highhanded swindling."[1] One witness, Agnes Jenkins, testified that under Riker's influence her husband had left her and her baby: "I came home one day and found all my furniture gone. Riker and my husband were packing the silverware." She further claimed that one of Riker's principles was to make money in the easiest way possible, and that he taught his followers that "there is no such thing as stealing."[2]

The charges were eventually dismissed on a technicality, but one of the witnesses, Freida Schwarz, filed new allegations against Riker and his wife a few months later. Mrs. Schwarz charged that she and her husband were separated at the colony, that her children were taken from her and mistreated, and that Riker habitually broke up families when they became members of Holy City. The case received considerable publicity, especially after Mrs. Schwarz testified that she had undergone an abortion at Riker's insistence, that the sexual favors of women were shared by the community, and that children were beaten and underfed. Holy City claimed on its own behalf that some families were permitted to live together, and that the colony's conditions were open for inspection by the judge at any time. Members denied charges of cruelty to children, claiming that they were always well fed and never punished too severely.

Once again, owing to the timely death of Mrs. Schwarz, Riker managed to extricate himself legally, at the same time drawing more of the curious to Holy City to visit the zoo or have a meal or just read the

Radio station KFQU was part of Riker's touristy facade at Holy City. It was shut down by the Federal Communications Commission in the late 1920's for gross violations. (Courtesy of the San Francisco *Chronicle*)

California's Holy City

Eccentric Father Riker Rules 90 Subjects There, Guaranteeing 'Perfect Government ...A Heaven on This Earth'

Holy City, earthly paradise of Father W. E. Riker, the "Wise Man of the Far West," lies in a peaceful valley in Santa Clara county, Cal. Father Riker claims to have devised the world's most perfect system of government. His system would, he says, solve all economic, racial and social problems. The 90 residents pay no taxes under his government.

Wooden Santa Clauses at Holy City. Each has one of Father Riker's axioms printed on its stomach. Jews and Gentiles, he says, were meant to be rulers of the world. He urges all white men to unite under a single flag, and he preaches suppression of Negroes and Orientals, who, he says are their inferiors.

The Wise Man. Father Riker describes himself as "the only man on earth who has complete wisdom, yet has never had a teacher or been guilty of reading books on the subject." Father Riker was born in California. He left school after the fourth grade. He arrived at his philosophy in 1908, "the year Halley's Comet appeared." It was not until 1919, however, that he founded Holy City. A ginger ale factory, religious peep shows and other businesses support his city.

Scenes From the Bible may be seen inside these little churches for a penny. All money taken from enterprises in the city is put in the common bank . . . Father Riker believes that only "white men" should be Christians. It is a sin to teach Christianity to Negroes and Orientals, he says. They should be taught only "Whitemanism."

Signs at Father Riker's Headquarters in Holy City. Father Riker's system calls for government control of all industry. Everyone is to have employment and security. To finance its program, the government would require all citizens to put their money in the government bank. Citizens would be allowed to draw out money, but no one would be allowed to hoard his wealth.

Float Used in Propaganda Parades. Father Riker's philosophy recognizes the Jewish race as the embodiment of God, and Christianity as a worship of the Jews by Gentiles. He considers himself Christ's Gentile successor.

By 1937 Holy City's bizarre attractions claimed attention from feature syndicates around the world. (Courtesy of the San Francisco *Chronicle*)

Riker's garage for his Fleetwood Cadillac is indicative of much of the ornate building style of Holy City. (Photograph by Paul Kagan)

signs and fill their gas tanks. The community was almost completely dependent on tourist trade, since it grew almost none of its own food. All community property was held in Riker's name. The colony supplied housing, furniture, clothing, and food to its members, who in turn did all the work, building, and maintenance yet received nothing except the necessities of life. Colony government was completely in Riker's hands. Living quarters were segregated by sex, no children were born, and Riker was content to leave the perpetuation of Holy City in the hands of God.

Riker's religion was peculiarly childish and in a sense nonreligious, as it was based on an essentially political idea: that the world belongs to the white race "to bless and to eternally and peacefully rule, for the good of all mankind."[3] Riker wrote copiously in defense of the "Great White Race" but did not consider himself prejudiced:

Any person who dares accuse me of racial prejudice . . . I will have to accuse him of being an educated fool with a ruptured brain or he may have an infantile or paralitic brain and is 100% stupid, non-progressive, non-intelligent, anti-Christ, and besides all of this he is as blind as a bat and in my opinion, he was mentally born up-side-down. . . . Here is what I claim to be, a 100% Spirit of California, God's country intelligent citizen."[4]

Riker was fond of metaphor and often identified the white race with the sun, and the other races with the planets, the servants of the sun. He also used the analogy of the human body, calling the trunk the gentiles, the head the Jews, the arms the Orientals, and the legs the blacks. Thus he would attempt to show that the subservience of the yellow and black races to the white was as natural and God-ordained as the subservience of a planet to its sun or the legs and arms to the body.

Women were also the object of some philosophizing by Riker. He believed women to be the vehicle whereby man might return to God:

Fake, small-appearing feet, which French heeled shoes and pinched toes develop, have a great power to make a man look down, which means to get down to sex. Small-footed women have a fascination over man to escape the delay in progression which big feet indicate. Man was created in a woman's brain, and since he is under the Divine Law to move forward he must move his interest from a woman's feet and get past them—complete his cycle—where he can feast of her through her head and brain which is typical of returning to the Garden of Eden, the holy place waiting for him. . . . Typically speaking, woman is an empty shell, and man is that something that

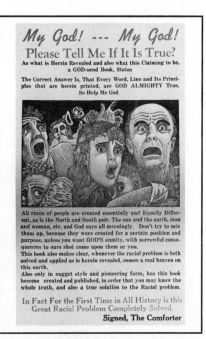

The Holy City Press, prolific in expounding Riker's racial theories, drew on the talents of artist Basil G. Wolverton, who later became an illustrator for *Mad* magazine. (Courtesy of the Bancroft Library)

As if in answer to the preceding pamphlet's question, "Please Tell Me If It Is True?" this 1947 polemic addressed to the "White Race People of this World" proclaimed "YES! YES!—IT IS TRUE." (Courtesy of the Bancroft Library)

Woman Sues Cult King for $500,000 in Love Tangle

Riker thrived on publicity. In this case he seems to have enjoyed the honeymoon without the marriage. Evelyn Rosencrantz was never able to prove her charges. (Courtesy of the San Francisco *Chronicle*)

has crawled out, and he must return and live, otherwise he will have no protection.[5]

Since Riker claimed to understand the nature and purpose of women, there is substantial irony in the fact that women made a great deal of trouble for him during the course of his career. Particularly effective was Evelyn Rosencrantz, an aviatrix, a forger, and an inmate at San Quentin Prison in 1928 when she made headlines by bringing a $500,000 breach of promise suit against Riker. She claimed that he had not only lived with her and promised to marry her but had also promised to finance her in an airplane flight from Holy City to Rome and star her in a philosophical film to be called *The Ideal Woman*. Mrs. Rosencrantz described the cottage she had shared with Riker in Palm City, California, and said she was expecting his child. She said he had told her that he had never been legally married to Lucille, and that his only real wife was Bessie Riker, then in an insane asylum.

Mother Lucille, back at Holy City, told the press that the story was a lie and the result of a sick mind.

She said her husband was at Holy City during the time Mrs. Rosencrantz claimed he was at Palm City with her; however, Mother Lucille was unable to indicate his whereabouts at the time she was questioned.

Mrs. Rosencrantz may have been attempting to get herself out of San Quentin (where she was serving a life term under the habitual criminal act after her fifth arrest for bad checks) with her story, for she certainly did not spare sensational details. Shortly after her initial suit was filed, she accused Riker of murdering a woman named Margaret White, who had known certain information about Riker with which she had been blackmailing him. Mrs. Rosencrantz said she saw Riker strangle Mrs. White in Culver City in December, 1927, after which he buried the body in quicklime near Holy City. Mrs. Rosencrantz claimed further that Riker had maneuvered her into jail, by secretly withdrawing money from her checking account so that her checks would bounce, because of her knowledge of this crime. She also accused Riker of being responsible for the death of Freida Schwarz, the chief witness against him in the morals case of 1921. Mrs. Rosencrantz alleged that Riker fed Mrs. Schwarz typhoid germs. Records of the San Francisco hospital where she died, however, showed that she strangled herself in delirium with an electric cord. The coroner's verdict was that she committed suicide while mentally deranged. Mrs. Rosencrantz claimed that immoral practices were part of Holy City's philosophy, and it was not difficult to find statements by Riker to support her charges: "Devil Worshipping is evolved God Worship,"[6] or, simply, "God winks his eye at any act we care to do if we take him in on the deal."[7]

Both Father Riker and Mother Lucille continued to deny all aspects of Mrs. Rosencrantz's story; Riker admitted he knew her but said he had never heard of Margaret White. Mother Lucille stated positively that her husband had never returned to Holy City with a body in his car. Mrs. Rosencrantz was never able to prove any part of her story, and finally interest died down.

Riker's vastly increased notoriety as a result of the Rosencrantz publicity makes one wonder why people continued to be drawn to him. He claimed to have the solutions to all of mankind's problems, but he was unable to keep himself out of trouble on even the most mundane levels. At about the same time as the Rosencrantz affair, Holy City's radio station, KFQU, was banned from the air for not operating in the public interest and deviating from its assigned frequency. Riker was also cited for reckless driving in 1928 and was involved in a series of nine automobile accidents

One of the Depression-style houses built during the thirties to house members of the Holy City community. (Photograph by Paul Kagan)

During Riker's numerous campaigns for governor his "Headquarters for the World's Perfect Government" offered up to $25,000 to anyone who could detect a flaw in his system. (Courtesy of Laura DeWitt James)

This view of Holy City depicts the virtue of "White Race" women. (Courtesy of Laura DeWitt James)

The Holy City peep show. (Courtesy of the San Francisco *Chronicle*)

in 1929 (he always drove new Cadillacs and sometimes used a black chauffeur). These may be insignificant incidents in the life of an ordinary man, but what about a man who called himself The Comforter and "a great shepherd watching over the people"?[8]

Was his appeal religious, or was it really based on the political premise of the scapegoat? As Hitler used the Jews as scapegoats, Riker used anyone who was not white. He entered the political arena quite openly, claiming to have found the secret of perfect government, which he was willing to tell anyone who would listen. In 1935 he publicly offered President Franklin D. Roosevelt a sure cure for the Depression which involved a "money-bouncing" plan with guaranteed results. Riker swore he would walk twenty miles on his crutches (recently acquired in another of his accidents) if anyone could prove his economic scheme unworkable, and he backed his statement with a $10,000 reward. Riker described his plan:

The Government takes over all banks with full access to all the money, and the people who are not privately employed will be employed immediately by the Government, as there is no limit to the amount of work that is needed to be done everywhere.

All money that is paid out will lawfully find its way back into the Government banks—thus providing a natural, perpetual circulation of the people's funds, with taxation of property and private insurance no longer needed.

The Government has full access to all unused money in the banks without interest, and all unused property without interference. All unused money of every citizen must be deposited in the Government bank for safekeeping, to be drawn out only for business or immediate use as needed.[9]

Riker was so impressed with his ideas that in 1937 he launched the first of his four campaigns for governor. The American party platform included tax revision, control of unfair business competition, a state banking and health insurance system, control of crime, state control of horse-racing and games of chance, state regulation of resources, more liberal divorce laws, and preferential employment of Californians.

His campaign literature, which poured unendingly from the Holy City Press, was virulently racist:

All you have to do in making people foolishly believe that an educated dog, Negro or Oriental is no different than the white race people, is to dress them up and educate them as are the white race people; and also with a white race man's name pinned to Mr. and Mrs. something, but in reality they are just what they are, which is the same as those where GOD put them, (inferior creatures in position), and don't forget it.

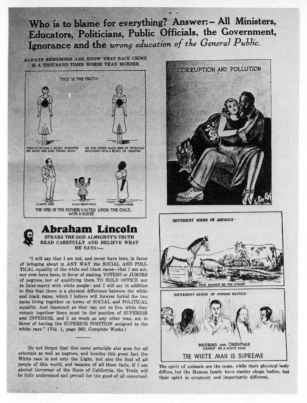

A graphic depiction of Riker's views on miscegenation. (Courtesy of the Bancroft Library)

He envisioned a "Racial Royal Family plan of government, where the exalted Jewish and Gentile people as a whole will become as a Royal King and Queen family of God in taking care of all its people and this entire world."

Riker compared the role of governor to that of a father:

What a good father will not stand for in his home, neither will I stand for as Governor in your own home State of California, where the trouble is.... If you were a father of a home, you wouldn't allow thieves and grafters to steal everything, nor would you allow negroes and orientals to impose, pollute, insult, undermine and get fresh with your wives and daughters.... We wouldn't make servants out of our own children, and since negroes and orientals cannot be our children, their only place is servants in our White Man's home and country.

He followed this campaign statement with a sonorous denunciation of all the other candidates as "Billygoats, Swelled up Bullfrogs, Devils, Big Mouth Bla! Bla!"

Riker was willing to send full-blooded blacks back to Africa, "where God wants them to be," if they wished to go. Once there, he predicted, they would "shrink back into their former head-hunting low-grade human wild man rhinocerous eating tactics." People of mixed race he regarded as "no different than mules," the living embodiment of "the unforgivable sins of the parents, visited upon the child." He felt, however, that they should remain in America, kept "under control to do the work." Riker offered to take all authority and business possessions away from nonwhites, eliminating "unfair competition."

Riker wanted to throw nonwhites out of the church as well:

It is absolutely true, that only our Great Creative Gentile White race of people have an absolute monopoly on Christianity, yet all others are allowed to receive blessings from us Christians and in the near future, it will be publicly announced, that negroes and orientals will be given a new religion, because their present original belief is worthless, the same as nothing, because it does nothing for them. As every one knows, they have to cater to us White race people for intellectual help. . . . The Christian White man means as much to negroes and orientals as does Christ mean to the Intelligent White Man. Therefore, "WHITEMANISM" is the only true religion for them.

Having resolved the economic and religious questions of race, Riker addressed himself to the cultural aspects in a pamphlet horrendously illustrated with grotesque faces drawn by Basil G. Wolverton, who later worked for *Mad* magazine:

Also mistakenly through some of our ignorant and sinful White Race people that try to improve those God-forsaken creatures of this Earth, have only made them worse off Spiritually, and they also try to ease off their insane sounding musical instruments, which also should not be allowed, because it only adds in them to have a contrary nature to be a far greater enemy to both: God, themselves and also to the Great White race of people. GOD SAYS, they must keep their HANDS OFF.

Riker regarded the following as the biological pièce de résistance:

The sex force of a Negro is not the same as is the White race man, that will naturally create a beautiful blue eyed, golden-haired baby; and not one of those kinky-haired non-creative black babies with a foul smell attached to it, and also with a likewise black spirit that has to prevail in them to cause them to be what they are.

Shortly after Riker's first political campaign, the Depression finally caught up with Holy City, which had been flourishing throughout the 1930's by offering penny-arcade attractions to tourists brought in by the highway that ran along its main street. Partly to destroy Holy City, a new state highway was built just before World War II which diverted traffic around the colony, eliminating its primary source of revenue. Desperate for a new method of attracting tourists,

Riker announced plans in October, 1939, to rebuild the colony into a single tower, made in the form of a beautiful woman sitting on top of the Santa Cruz Mountains. The tower-woman would be as large as the Colossus of Rhodes, with twelve elevators inside.

Riker's energies were turned from this project, however, when he was arrested in 1942 on sedition charges. The Federal Bureau of Investigation seized fifteen cases of documents at Holy City, including letters from Riker to Hitler. Riker, who had always called himself a friend of the Jews, had received an answer from Hitler's secretary expressing "limited approval" of his ideas, according to the F.B.I. The F.B.I. also cited a pamphlet in which Riker described Hitler as a "second Martin Luther, freeing the people from the ownership of the international banker."[10] The formal charges included impairing the morale of the armed forces through conversations with certain soldiers in which Riker advocated seeking a peace with the Axis, except for Japan. Ironically enough, a Japanese propaganda broadcast expressed sympathy for Riker as a "persecuted Catholic priest," to the amusement of the San Francisco press, which pointed out that Riker considered the Japanese to be "slimy, abominable reptiles."[11]

Riker, sixty-eight years old at the time of his arrest, appeared in court with an American flag tucked into his breast pocket and sat immobile with his wife and followers as the prosecution read from copies of his letters to Hitler: "Your opportunity is now ripe . . . and when it is done, you will prove yourself to be the greatest character that has ever lived since the time of Jesus Christ. A little meditation on your part and you will be the great emancipator of Europe."[12] During the course of the well-publicized trial Riker took the stand in his own defense and said he believed himself to be the greatest man in the world after Benjamin Franklin and Abraham Lincoln, a man who held the "true solution of all problems—to stop Jewish persecution and to establish peace."

Riker's attorney was Melvin Belli, whose strategy displayed the grandstand techniques that were to make him famous. A few days after the opening of the trial, in December, 1942, Belli filed an affidavit in federal court charging that Father Divine, messiah to thousands of blacks in Harlem, had inspired the arrest of Riker out of jealousy. According to the attorney: "Father Divine is jealous because Father Riker has used the name 'Father' and calls himself 'The Wise Man of the West,' whereas Father Divine claimed he is the one wise man, and, in fact, claims he is God."[13] Belli did not mention that in one of his pamphlets Riker had called Father Divine an "American

" 'Father' Riker Faces Sedition Trial, 12/1/42. A jury of six men and six women was chosen in San Francisco Dec. 1 for the Federal court trial of William E. (Father) Riker, left, on charges of Sedition. Riker is accompanied by his attorney, Melvin Belli. Testimony will begin Dec. 7." (Courtesy of Wide World Photos)

THE TWO GREAT MEN *of* GOD

WHO are divinely functioning in a spiritual, wise and Divine Wedlock as herein explained, that challenges and defies the Elite of this world to successfully dispute their herein printed New statements and Perfect Philosophy and Plans.

Father William E. Riker   *King David Aaron*

The Promised Comforter   *The New Jewish Messiah*

THE WHOLE TRUTH AND NOTHING BUT THE TRUTH SO HELP ME GOD IS HEREIN PRINTED

All of this happened, because of time, spiritual development and fulfillment of the Divine Plan, which means it is the Will and Law of GOD (that is now) coming into tangible expression. In other words it is the fulfillment of the Divine and true purpose of the Great Jewish people, and also the true spirit and workings of Christianity coming into this world in full bloom, in order that all mankind may now have Eternal Life and Peace on this Earth, including all of the good things that go with it. Reading this book is like reading what was left out of other books. and the bible.

READ THIS LEAFLET CAREFULLY AND YOU WILL BECOME SPIRITUALLY ENLIGHTENED FOR THE FIRST TIME.

Riker in 1956 with his "new Jewish Messiah," Maurice Kline, who ultimately wrested control of Holy City from Riker and sold it to land developers. (Courtesy of the Bancroft Library)

witch doctor; a half-witted, big-mouth rhinocerous"; instead, Belli accused Father Divine of spreading false reports that Riker persecuted blacks. Belli asked to have Father Divine brought to California as a witness and promised that Riker would sue Father Divine for libel and slander as soon as the trial was over. Belli said Riker was guilty of "no other charge than being too enthusiastic and too outspoken an American," citing Riker's promise of a $500 war bond to the first American pilot to bomb Tokyo. Meanwhile, Riker, described by a *Chronicle* reporter as "a bumbling, sweat-peppered old man," swore that "since Pearl Harbor I have been a real warrior, doing all in my power to demonstrate my Americanism."[14]

Belli's closing argument to the jury was so moving that Riker himself wept. Belli presented his client as a "pitiful and pathetic" man, "guilty of many things but not seditious," and won an acquittal on all counts. An ironic footnote to the strange case is that Belli had to sue Riker to collect his fee.

The postwar years saw the further decline of Holy City. In 1948 the *Chronicle* published a long, retrospective article that offered an explanation of Holy City's changing fortunes, starting with Riker's initial success:

The idea was very simple. Simply come to Holy City and bring your dough. Then you can stop worrying about life and taxes and traffic tickets and your money, too. Just eat and sleep and do a little work when you feel like it. Let the Comforter do the worrying.

Riker got plenty of converts. Simple people who were confused by life and afraid of the future. He put them to work in one of his many enterprises, permitted them to eat and sleep in one of his shanties, and gave them plenty of philosophy. . . . Then things got tough. The mean old state diverted the main highway away from Holy City. . . . Today, the business establishments have gone to pot, and the hundreds of signs are cracking and peeling and falling apart. . . . The radio station is empty and forlorn. . . . A mere twenty of the original two hundred converts remain in the colony, and most of these totter, vacant eyed and cane supported, through the deserted village.

Mother Lucille died in 1950, but Riker continued to cast around for ways to inject some new life into Holy City. He turned to unexpected quarters to get it: Maurice Kline, former Hollywood music director of the radio program *Sergeant Preston of the Yukon*, became the "Jewish Messiah" of Holy City in 1956. Riker gave Kline a half-interest in Holy City's property and expected in return that Kline would rebuild and promote the colony. Kline promised Riker that Holy City would soon be able to boast a freeway, a lake, an airport, a private railroad, and an outdoor amphi-

Holy City ca. 1939, nestled comfortably in the Santa Cruz Mountains, with the Holy City Press at the upper center and the Holy City Market to its right. (Courtesy of the San Francisco *Chronicle*)

August 31, 1959: "Jerusalem ablaze—Two-thirds of the 'New Jerusalem' built by 'Father' William Riker at Holy City . . . lies in ashes today." (Courtesy of the San Francisco *Chronicle*)

theater. New pamphlets were issued, announcing Holy City to be "Headquarters of the world's leader and comforter and the Jewish Messiah." Riker even came up with a "philosophy of the nerves . . . 100 percent Brand New, All-wise and Strictly Up-to-date" to embellish Holy City's revamped image.

By February, 1959, Riker and Kline were battling over the ownership of Holy City. After Riker had given Kline half-ownership, Kline persuaded Riker and his eight aging disciples to sell him the other half in exchange for a thousand dollars a year each, payable in food, lodging, and medical care, which was what they had already been receiving free for forty years. Then Riker demanded Holy City back and went to court, charging that Kline had fraudulently misrepresented himself, and that his interest in the colony was purely financial. Kline replied that Riker had lured him away from his well-paying Hollywood job, and that he had tried to accept Riker's teachings but found it difficult because they changed so often. Riker lost, the judge finding that there had been no wrongdoing on Kline's part, and Kline gained control of Holy City's property. Riker and those who had followed him so long were reduced to the role of boarders on someone else's land.

By the early 1960's Kline removed himself from the Holy City enterprise by selling the land to a development company. The company, however, failed to implement any plans for the acreage, and Riker and his ancient followers managed to stay on. Most of the news to come out of Holy City in the 1960's concerned Robert Clogher, a relative newcomer to Riker's fading kingdom, who was continually running for office on the nudist ticket. Clogher also publicly appealed to the prostitutes of California to donate a tenth of their income to help him save Holy City from "infidels and unbelievers."[15]

In 1966, at the age of ninety-four Riker became a Roman Catholic. "I was intelligently converted," he said. "I've been living a celibate life for ten years." In 1967, the "summer of love" in San Francisco, Clogher invited the hippies to Holy City. "We hold," he said, "that 100,000 hippies . . . would be a great asset to Holy City, what with our population having dwindled sharply over the past decade or so. Further, 100,000 hippies, were they to arrive in Holy City on the Pentecost, might provide a miracle, that is, the resurrection of the holy ghost town of Holy City." But none came.

On December 3, 1969, Riker died in Agnews State Hospital in San Jose, after spending time in a series of other mental hospitals. Ironically, in better days Riker used to take mental cases from these hospitals and put them to work in his colony, in return for which they received care and shelter.

Riker's house at Holy City still stands—ramshackle and inhabited by a man known in the neighborhood as Crazy Harry—along with a few of the other old buildings and a few new ones, although plans for the development of the area have not yet been realized. The wooden Santa Claus figures that lined the main street are gone, but a few of the cryptic signs are stacked in a garage, guarded by Crazy Harry.

Holy City today, deserted for several years, constitutes a continuous fire hazard. (Photograph by Paul Kagan)

Cranking up one of Llano del Rio's two trucks in 1915. (Courtesy of Bernie Stevens and Jean Nourse)

CHAPTER 7

Llano del Rio

In 1914 the Llano del Rio Co-operative Colony was founded by a handful of visionary California socialists about forty-five miles north of Los Angeles. Based on the principles of equal ownership, equal wages, and equal social opportunities, Llano was meant to demonstrate practically that cooperation could work. Men and women came to Llano to leave behind their worries about job insecurity, unemployment, and the chaos of crime and pollution spawned by the great cities.

Llano's principal founder, Job Harriman, grew up on an Indiana farm and was trained for the ministry, but he rejected religion for the study of law. He was later described by Aldous Huxley as "a Marxist lawyer with a Gladstone collar and the face of a revivalist or a Shakespearean actor."[1] Harriman moved to California in 1886 and became a socialist around 1890. During the 1890's he was increasingly attracted to the utopian movement. He joined a Nationalist club and also became interested in Altruria, a short-lived California community inspired by William Dean Howells's 1894 novel, *A Traveler from Altruria*. For twenty years Harriman was active in socialist politics. He was a Vice-Presidential candidate on a ticket headed by Eugene Debs in 1900 and came close to being elected mayor of Los Angeles in 1911. A major issue in the latter campaign was the case of the radical McNamara brothers, who were accused of bombing

the Los Angeles *Times* building. Harriman supported the brothers' cause, but a few days before the election they confessed to the crime, firmly ending any chance Harriman had of winning.

Turning from politics, Harriman decided to start a colony. A site in the Antelope Valley was chosen for the location of the community after a long search. An earlier colony of temperance advocates had completed some of the work necessary to irrigate the land, which Harriman and his supporters were able to buy at a low price. The original down payment may have been only five dollars.

Harriman reorganized the temperance colony's Mescal Water and Land Company into the Llano del Rio Company of California and began selling company stock late in 1913 by advertising in the socialist press. The company issued two million shares of stock, valued at $1 each. Membership required the purchase of two thousand shares. Members were asked to make a down payment of $500, but this was later changed to $750; the balance was paid at the rate of $1 a day out of the $4-a-day wages the colony offered. These wages were never actually paid the members, but almost no one cared. Walter Millsap, a long-time member of the colony, described the results:

They made the colossal blunder of selling stock according to the ordinary method—you get a fiscal agent, and he goes out and sells stock for a commission. The agent promised everything under the sun and heaven on earth if they'd sign on the dotted line and give him five hundred dollars. Why, they could just live in paradise from then on. It wasn't quite paradise. . . . All the bookkeeping systems broke down; all the meal-ticket systems fell down. But everyone knew whether the other fellow was doing his part or whether he was sick, and they just dumped the whole thing in the ashcan and went to the table and ate dinner.[2]

Llano opened on May Day, 1914, with five families, five pigs, a team of horses, and a cow. By early 1915 membership had grown to 150, and there were a hundred cows and as many hogs. According to an early Llano colonist, Ernest S. Wooster, who at one time was manager of the Llano publication program,

the problem of housing became so important that other work had to be dropped to care for this pressing necessity. . . . Incoming people were finally put into tents for the most part, and the canvas village of Llano covered a population of devoted idealists determined to demonstrate the success and practicability of their principles. A little later houses of adobe were built, the brick being moulded in hard moulds the usual size of commercial brick, and laid in the ordinary way.[3]

Besides the houses, the other structures eventually included a hotel, two barns, a concrete silo, a dairy, an office building, a cannery, and two industrial buildings. In addition, the colonists laid miles of irrigation ditches and planted 240 acres of alfalfa and 200 acres of orchards.

For as long as the cash lasted, times were good, enthusiasm high and achievement correspondingly great. A wagon road was driven through the foothills, up into the timberland of the San Gabriel Mountains. Trees were felled and laboriously brought down to the sawmill in the plain, below. A quarry was opened, a lime kiln constructed. The tents of the first colonists gave place to shacks, the shacks to houses. Next a hotel was built, to accommodate the interested visitors from the infernal regions of capitalism. Schools and workshops appeared as though by magic. Irrigation ditches were dug and lined. Eighty horses and a steam tractor cleared, leveled, plowed and harvested. Fruit trees were planted, pears canned, alfalfa cut and stored, cows milked and "the West's most modern rabbitry" established.[4]

By 1917, according to Wooster, the Llano industries included

a print shop, shoe shop, laundry, cannery, clothes cleaning, warehouse, machine shop, blacksmith shop, rug making, planing mill, range stock, hog raising, dairy goats, soap

An early call to join the colony, from *The Western Comrade*, June, 1914.

Marxist lawyer Job Harriman, with "the face of a revivalist or a Shakespearean actor," promoted Llano del Rio as a viable example of the workability of socialism. (Courtesy of the Huntington Library)

Lacking capital resources, the colony often had to re-imburse its members in services rather than cash. The meal-ticket was a fixture of the labor-exchange program. (Kagan Collection, California Historical Society Library)

A carload of new colonists, with their luggage roped to the running board, arrives at the main entrance on Llano Boulevard. New residents were a mixed blessing. Although each new family contributed a small nest egg to the general fund, it also added more mouths to be fed from the colony's limited food stocks. (Kagan Collection, California Historical Society Library)

A chill blanket of snow emphasizes the bleak setting of the colony, located in the Mojave Desert at the eastern base of the San Gabriel Mountains, twenty miles from Palmdale. At the time of this photograph, January, 1917, most of the original tent houses were still in use. (Courtesy of Bernie Stevens and Jean Nourse)

making, lumbering, publishing newspaper and magazine, bakery, fish hatchery, transportation, barber shop, over-alls and shirt making, paint shop, lime kiln, dairy, cabinet shop, nursery, alfalfa, orchards, poultry, gardens, rabbitry, and brick making.[5]

The colony at that time numbered over a thousand. New arrivals brought needed cash but also more mouths to feed.

The colonists were troubled by poor and monoto-nous food—sometimes carrots were the only vegetable —and by inadequate shelter. The adobe houses they built melted in the desert rain. A twelve-year-old girl wrote one winter: "We had the awfulest rain and wind that I have even seen. It blew the top of the hotel porch off and part of the dining room. It blew many of the tents down. . . . Our tent leaks awful."[6]

Perhaps in reaction to these conditions the colonists often wasted time and energy on get-rich-quick schemes. One man planned an airplane that would be within the price range of most families. He built a model for it on an empty patch of Llano land, but when it was furnished, he was so afraid of testing it that he set it on fire instead, although he claimed it was an accident. Other colonists prospected for gold, and still others listened to a man who claimed to be a water witch. They dug a number of dry wells before

they relinquished their belief in the willow wand. There was a man who believed in turnips as a cash crop but never planted any, and there was a Mr. Gibbons who always complained about how things were run but was always too sick to do any work. Through subsequent years at Llano, slackers were called Gibbonites.

The colonists may have lived largely on carrots and dreams, but they often found ways to have a good time. Harriman emphasized "equal social opportunities," and colony dances, open to outside visitors, were held weekly. Harriman cherished and shared his plan for Llano as the city of the future, ten thousand strong, with five-room houses for every family. Pursuing this vision, Llanoites lost sight of more mundane problems and were surprised when the California commissioner of corporations condemned the colony for putting waste in its water supply and for profiteering at their cooperative store. The Llano del Rio Company quickly issued an ordinance: "It shall be unlawful for any person residing in this colony to bathe, wade, puddle, or play in, or in any manner to pollute or contaminate the waters."

After the commissioner's investigation Harriman was faced with mutiny and retained control only through a legal maneuver—he established a new Llano del Rio Company in Nevada and used its stock

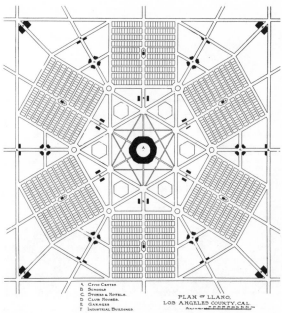

A map of the proposed city of Llano, from *The Western Comrade* of March, 1915. The city was to include a civic center, schools, stores, hotels, clubhouses, garages, and industrial buildings. It was never realized.

Application for Membership
in the
Llano Del Rio Co-operative Colony

Only industrious men and women of high ideals and constructive ideas with reputations for good citizenship are desirable members of the LLANO DEL RIO CO-OPERATIVE COLONY. If you are willing to put your whole ability and spirit into this enterprise, to work in harmony with your fellow co-operators, and to abide by the rules adopted, you will be cordially welcomed as part of this noble enterprise.

☐ Do you believe in the profit system?

☐ What should be done with an article that evidently was lost by someone?

☐ Will solving the economic problem ultimately lead to solving the social problem?

☐ Is happiness a state of mind or dependent upon affluent material conditions?

☐ Do you believe in a peaceful settlement of ALL misunderstandings?

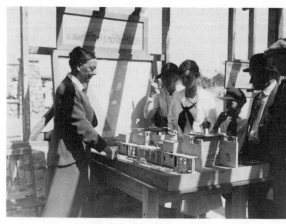

A. Constance Austin showing a model of the ideal planned socialist city in the half-finished men's dormitory, which was constructed of fieldstones and timber. (Kagan Collection, California Historical Society Library)

An exhortation from *The Western Comrade*, August–September, 1916.

A grandiloquent plan for a central building which never got beyond the drawing board. A copy of this drawing hangs above Constance Austin's head in the preceding illustration. (Kagan Collection, California Historical Society Library)

The men's dormitory and the hotel at Llano in 1916. (Courtesy of the Los Angeles *Times*)

to buy all the California property. Llano became a Nevada corporation. Harriman's leadership, however, was often threatened by rebellious colonists:

There were the idealistic purists, who complained that he was making too many compromises with the devils of capitalism; there were the malingerers, who criticized but refused to work; there were the greedy with their clamor for special privileges; there were the power-lovers who envied him and were ambitious to take his place.[7]

Harriman began his colony with the firm belief that "the hearts and minds of men would be as sweet and gentle and loving as in babyhood, if the stream of life were not polluted by the vicious methods of the universal conflict of interests."[8] The results of his experiment did not strengthen his belief. In 1924 he wrote:

Men and women would gather around the fire in the large hotel room of an evening and discuss the various phases of socialism as they had imagined them. . . . And yet these very same people when in the shop or field would act as differently as they would have acted had they never heard of socialism.

Some were selfish, arrogant, and egotistical and shirked their duties, quit early, went to work late, rested often, talked much, criticized everything and everybody, wanted the lion's share at the commissary, wanted the best houses, with extra furniture, neglected the animals, were careless with tools, and did everything that might be thought of by those who were seeking the advantage of those about them. . . . The selfish persisted in their course with a persistence that was amazing.[9]

The colony directors once threatened to post the names of all those who failed to work as "parasites," but the selfish at Llano still persisted in their course, often exploiting their general assembly, which was intended as an expression of the freedom allowed the colonists:

It was Democracy rampant, belligerent, unrestricted; an inquisition, a mental pillory, a mad house of meddlesomeness and attempts at business, a jumble of passions and idealism—and all in deadly earnest. . . . It became a Frankenstein which threatened to destroy the colony. It was the fruit of the propaganda for democracy of the early soap-boxers, but these street-corner orators had utterly failed to define what democracy means. The General Assembly was democracy with the lid off.[10]

Factionalism became so extreme that one man complained that although he had a sick child, his adobe house was not completed, because he was not "standing with the right crowd."

One minority group within the colony began holding secret meetings in the sagebrush at night. They called themselves the Welfare League and demanded an even more extreme form of democracy than the general assembly provided: a popular vote to be taken on every plan before it was put into effect. "The 'democrats' were offered the alfalfa industry to be operated experimentally by them according to their democratic notions. If their plan proved to be all they claimed for it, other industries were to be shifted one by one."[11] The entire colony met to discuss the plan. The members of the Welfare League came in wearing sagebrush pinned to their clothing as a symbol of their organization and rejected the plan. Harriman expelled their leaders from the colony and the insurrection ended, but "brush gang" remained in the language of Llano, referring to those "chronically and unreasonably disgruntled."[12]

An article in the Llano promotional magazine, *The Western Comrade,* attempted to discourage the arrival of more potential brush-gangers:

Those who imagine, as some of our newcomers do, that a complete revolution of the methods of getting must immediately obtain upon their arrival here, are due for a shock. We are not attempting an Utopian phantasmagoria, but are constantly dealing with things of life, nature and harness and horses, plows, wood cutting and the building of homes.[13]

Llano might have survived the quarrels among its members, but it was faced with a problem much more severe—the problem of how the colony's expanding membership could live off its barren land.

In a good year (and every other year is bad) water from the Big Rock Creek makes possible the raising, at Llano, of crops and cattle worth perhaps a hundred thousand dollars. The Colony owned rights to part of this water. On its irrigated acres fifty, or at the most, a hundred persons might have eked out a precarious living. But by the beginning of 1917 Harriman had accepted the applications of almost a thousand eager co-operators. . . . As the situation grew worse, the propagandists became more lyrical. "Llano offers hope and inspiration for the masses. . . . Its purpose is to solve unemployment, to assure safety and comfort for the future and old age." And the words were accompanied by a detailed plan of the city which was just about to be built. . . . The publicity worked. Applications and, more important, checks kept steadily coming in. With each arrival of an idealist's life savings, there was a respite. But a respite at a price. For with those life-savings came another member and his family.[14]

In the midst of its financial difficulties Llano was betrayed by one of its own officers. Gentry Purviance McCorkle, secretary of the colony, "brought the hopes of the California enterprise to an end. What would undoubtedly have developed into a substantial and valuable estate was made a failure because of the grasping short sightedness of one who considered his own interests first and did not hesitate to use the most unscrupulous means."[15] McCorkle told the story in his unpublished autobiography, "Wayside Memories of a Tennessee Rebel":

During 1916 I began to see that the colony was slipping. . . . In order to protect my investment, I organized the Llano Investment Company. . . . I then transferred to this company various properties that had not been mortgaged and also the colony notes for money owed me. I did not issue all of the stock, just . . . 50% to myself.[16]

McCorkle considered Llano a lost cause because of a conflict over water rights between the colony members

The back cover from *The Western Comrade* of June, 1915.

Children were expected to help in sowing seeds for future crops. The colony's agricultural production was remarkably successful. During its first year the colony produced 75 percent of the food it consumed, and by 1916 it was producing about 90 percent. Before the group disbanded, it had more than two thousand acres of alfalfa, corn, truck crops, and pear trees. One of the most abundant crops was carrots—a vegetable that the colonists came to know altogether too well. (Photograph by Walter Millsap, Kagan Collection, California Historical Society Library)

The bulging load of No. 10 cans on Llano's second truck attests to the volume of goods produced by the cannery. (Courtesy of Bernie Stevens and Jean Nourse)

and the neighboring citizens of the Big Rock Water District. Llano went to court over the right to irrigate its acres. The opposing attorney spoke of "socialistic plunderers," and the case was lost. McCorkle believed the decision rendered the land valueless—"nothing but jack rabbits and stink weeds"—and he moved to protect himself. McCorkle's financial manipulations, which forced Llano into bankruptcy proceedings in which the court closed the colony, precipitated a plan Harriman had long considered: moving Llano to a new location.

In the summer of 1917 Harriman learned of twenty thousand acres of land for sale by the Gulf Lumber Company in Louisiana. The land had been logged, but it included a small town. The lumber company's price of $125,000 payable over several years was accepted by the colony's directors in August. The original plan to maintain the orchards in California quickly faded, and all effort was poured into the new colony.

Girls prepare freshly harvested apples for canning (ca. 1916). (Photograph by Walter Millsap, Kagan Collection, California Historical Society Library)

There was another blissful dawn, followed by a prolonged struggle with a hundred ferocious Texans, who had been invited to join the community, but had not, apparently, been told that it was a co-operative. When these extremely rugged individualists had gone, taking with them most of the Colony's livestock and machinery, the survivors settled down to the dismal realities of life on an inadequate economic foundation. Work was hard, and for diversion

#10
cans for
lano Cannery

The
WESTERN
COMRADE

January - 1916   Five Cents

Preparedness Number

Printing was a major endeavor at Llano throughout its history, partly because of the abundance of socialist rhetoric generated in the colony. A printer (above) locks up the galleys of a letterpress publication for proofing. The printing plant also had sheet-fed offset equipment. Students from the Llano school (below) learned to operate a Linotype as part of their technical training. Quality standards were fairly high. Once in a while the plant outdid itself by producing work such as the two-color line drawing reproduced on the magazine cover at the left. (Photographs by Walter Millsap, Kagan Collection, California Historical Society Library)

A plaster-cast souvenir, of somewhat dubious aesthetic charms, depicts the joyful transformation of one Henry Dubb after he came to Llano. (Kagan Collection, California Historical Society Library)

This Goat Belongs to Llano Boys

They have a flock of goats, blooded Swiss milk stock. They have chickens, turkeys, rabbits, horses and pets. The boys are building a henhouse eighty feet long. They are building a club house one hundred and twelve feet long.

Does Your Boy Have this Chance?

Or Is He Roaming the Streets in Bad Company?

WHAT sort of a future are you planning for your children? What are your girls learning? Is their environment good? Are they spending their time profitably? Are they following healthful pursuits?

A membership for you will give them the opportunity they need. You can make them healthy, robust, happy. They will learn practicable things and develop as you would like to see them.

There is an opportunity for you and your family at Llano.

Its many developing industries offer your children the scope of opportunity that will permit them to select the occupation they prefer. They can make this selection by actual contact; each child gains a thorough understanding of the different lines of work.

And then above all is the freedom, the independence, the assurance of steady employment, the protection in old age. A membership in the Llano del Rio Colony is the only perfect insurance.

Write at once for "The Gateway to Freedom" and other descriptive literature

Llano Boys Have Their Own Livestock

Llano del Rio Colony

THE WORLD'S GREATEST CO-OPERATIVE COMMUNITY

Llano   Los Angeles County   California

Pushing a theme with an uncomfortably modern connotation, the Llano colony advertised in October, 1916, for families that were worrying even then about "street people." Note that the colony felt sufficiently self-confident by then to proclaim itself "The World's Greatest Co-operative Community."

there were only the weekly dances, the intrigues of several rival brush-gangs and the spectacle of the struggle for power between the ailing Harriman and an ex-insurance salesman of boundless energy, called George T. Pickett.[17]

Harriman, sick with tuberculosis and disillusioned with Llano, returned to California, where he died in 1925. Pickett, who became manager of the colony in 1924 and ruled with considerable authority until 1938, was a man fond of saying that he would "rather work with a bunch of morons than with a lot of over-educated kickers."[18] Pickett was interested in working with children and organized a gang of boys to repair the colony's roads. Within a few years he had formed a separate children's compound within the colony which offered adventure, work, and instruction to Llano's new generation. The children built their own classrooms and living quarters, grew their own vegetables, and took care of the goats. This school was known as the Kid Kolony.

The work the children do is not considered of great value; in fact it is the general opinion that much more could be achieved if the children did not have to be shown and were not there to waste materials and the time of adults. But the training of the children is sufficient reason for continuing the practice."[19]

When they were not toiling in the fields or arguing socialist doctrine, the Llanoites enjoyed themselves in a relaxed round of dances and socials, climaxed with the annual celebration of May Day. With all the flags and bunting of a Fourth of July celebration, the colony produced a memorable festival in 1917, featuring sack races, parades, concerts, and dramatics. The Llano band, ensconced on a bunting-draped platform, played patriotic and revolutionary tunes. (Photograph by Walter Millsap, Kagan Collection, California Historical Society Library)

The choral society, costumed for the 1917 May Day celebration, launches with gusto into a song. The favorite of the day was the "Marseillaise." (Photograph by Walter Millsap, Kagan Collection, California Historical Society Library)

After a barbecue supper, girls from the Llano school twirled around the Maypole. The evening was concluded by a performance by the dramatic club of *Mishaps of Minerva*, followed by dancing in the assembly hall. (Photograph by Walter Millsap, Kagan Collection, California Historical Society Library)

Jets of steam rise from standpipes at the soap factory (right), and a worker slices a raw block of soap into laundry cakes (above). Unfortunately, the plant consumed an undue volume of water and contributed to the critical water shortage. (Kagan Collection, California Historical Society Library)

Promises of life-long employment, such as this advertisement in *The Western Comrade* (November, 1915), attracted some colonists with more materialistic than idealistic goals who were reluctant to work industriously and hampered the colony's productivity.

Nathan and Phillip Elkins, son and grandson of Meyer Elkins, the Llano photographer. Nathan Elkins was a young boy at Llano. (Photograph by Paul Kagan)

Water was scarce and polluted. All that remains of the water system today is this dry fountain, baking in the desert sun. (Photograph by Paul Kagan)

Ditch-diggers pause in their labors to face the camera of Meyer Elkins, a colony photographer whose studio is visible at the left. Irrigation ditches were dug in anticipation of a dam on Big Rock Creek, but it was never constructed. (Courtesy of Bernie Stevens and Jean Nourse)

In spite of these efforts few of Llano's children wished to remain in the colony when they were old enough to choose:

Of those nineteenth-century communities which survived long enough to rear a second generation of co-operatives, few were able to resist the impact of the bicycle. Mounted on a pair of wheels, the young people were able to explore that unredeemed but fascinating world "on the outside." After each expedition, it was with mounting reluctance that they returned to the all too familiar crowd. In the end reluctance hardened into refusal. They went out one day and never came back.[20]

Pickett's interest in children did not cause him to neglect the adults. He abolished the general assembly in favor of a weekly "psychology" meeting, at which he gave inspiring talks on cooperative ideals. Members were encouraged to confess their sins against the community. The meetings became an effective instrument of control in Pickett's hands:

I'll never forget one Thursday when George [Pickett] stopped Tom's roustabout wagon hauling a load of fresh loaves from the bakery to the hotel for dinner and picked off an armful of golden loaves which he took home in his car for his own use, for the manager and his little family seldom ate with the herd. Then that night at his pet psychology meeting, where he harangued the half a hundred oldsters who attended regularly, he bawled out a co-operator of lesser stature for using a handful of colony nails for some private carpentering purpose.[21]

By 1926 there were factions in the colony violently opposed to Pickett's leadership. In 1927 the protesters filed suit against the Llano del Rio Company, charging that

the colony had reduced workers to peons in behalf of the Gulf Lumber Company, and that colonists were poorly fed, wretchedly clothed, and housed in typhus-infested mill huts. The colony schools, with their program of half-work and half-study, had prostituted small children to the nefarious purposes of Pickett . . . colony leaders had "advocated the social practice commonly known as 'free love.' "[22]

The end of the grand experiment: The colonists began to move out early in 1918. More than a hundred migrated to a new site in Louisiana. Scores of farm machines were left behind. The buildings were quickly sacked and stripped after the shutdown. (Courtesy of the Los Angeles *Times*)

Llano today: the ruins of a fieldstone house in southern California's dry desert sands. (Photograph by Paul Kagan)

The colony moved to Louisiana in late 1917 in hopes of finding more water and better conditions.

The colonists found suf-ficient water in Louisiana to warrant the construc-tion of these rowboats. Part of the mill town they purchased is visible in the background. (Pho-tograph by Walter Mill-sap, Kagan Collection, California Historical So-ciety Library)

Renaming the mill town New-llano, the colonists proceeded to build again. Here the "Kid Kolony" is under construction. (Photograph by Walter Millsap, Kagan Collection, California Historical Society Library)

A harnessed team of young Llanoites combined work and play in Louisiana. (Photograph by Walter Millsap, Kagan Collection, California Historical Society Library)

One of man's oldest occupations, the gathering of food. (Photograph by Walter Millsap, Kagan Collection, California Historical Society Library)

The charges of immorality were blatantly untrue and easily disproved. Pickett made his opponents look foolish over this issue in the early stages of the case and went on to win easily.

Llano limped along into the thirties, always in financial trouble and often torn by power struggles. By 1936 the colony had gone bankrupt. This catastrophe brought the warring factions together in a genuine attempt at cooperation which lasted two years, but in 1938 Llano finally failed, and its inhabitants dispersed. Although the Louisiana colony lasted for twenty-one years and the California experiment for only three, Llano's greatest monument lies in the Antelope Valley, where the ruined stone buildings reminded Aldous Huxley of Shelley's lines in "Ozymandias":

> Round the decay
> Of that colossal wreck, boundless and bare
> The lone and level sands stretch far away.

A profound dissatisfaction with the prevailing conditions of life was the original impetus for the founding of Llano del Rio, which was to be a constructive alternative to the woes and cares of life. Inside Llano, however, the same problems—indolence, avarice, envy, ignorance—appeared even more intensified than they had been in the "outside" world. What was missing that might have enabled Llano to continue in spite of the factions and frictions? Was there a basic misunderstanding about man and his dependence on other men, society, and the environment?

Llano's three-and-a-half-year existence in California did more than lay the basis for a comparatively long-lived nonspiritual community in the United States. Many Llanoites left the colony with a new and personal wisdom. Job Harriman, most of all, realized that fundamental human problems could not be solved by external social organization alone. Llano continues to bear fruit today as ex-Llanoites begin new social experiments in society and bring more understanding to the lives of their own families. Finally, Llano del Rio stands as an historical example, a compendium of data about communal living, for all those who are concerned today with the questions of community.

Percy Bysshe Shelley: "And on the pedestal these words appear: / 'My name is Ozymandias, king of kings: / Look on my works, ye Mighty, and despair!'" (Photograph by Paul Kagan)

Finis E. Yoakum and family around 1900. When Yoakum died, Charles and Finis, Jr. (standing), allowed the county authorities to drive the last resident out of Pisgah Grande and later sold the property. (Courtesy of H. J. Smith)

CHAPTER **8**

Pisgah Grande

Pisgah Grande was once an active commune of Christian evangelists. Today, these men and women who worked with the zeal and fervor of the Lord, who blessed handkerchiefs, spoke in tongues, and helped the sick and distressed, might be called Jesus freaks. Where did the energy and unshakable faith come from that inspired Finis Yoakum and his followers to hew a city out of the mountains? Religious zeal and proselytizing are often an attempt to convince others of that which one needs to prove for one's self. Still, there remains something strange and mysterious about the origins, life, and remains of this commune.

Pisgah Grande is now a rotting ghost town in a remote valley of southern California's Santa Susana Mountains. From 1914 to 1921, Pisgah Grande functioned as a Pentecostal Christian commune. The road to the town is not open to the public. A sign reads, "No tresspass. Have gun will shoot." But there is a caretaker-farmer in a cowboy hat who will unlock the gate and take a visitor up the long winding foothill road in his one-ton pickup.

Pisgah Grande was officially abandoned more than fifty years ago, but its buildings, scattered through the hills, are still full: broken glass, rusty tools, ancient appliances, a crumbling couch with ruffles and carved feet turned up to the ceiling. One deserted kitchen holds an icebox, cupcake tins, and other utensils,

probably left by squatters, along with a can of Libby's Vienna frankfurters.

A two-story brick house with a double fireplace is in a reasonably good state of preservation. The wicker lawn furniture outside seems to blend with the soil. A shower and sink are rigged in the yard. There is a 1960 magazine, an empty cartridge box, and fairly new tar-paper on the roof. It is clear that Pisgah continued to shelter lost souls long after its communal days were ended. A fugitive embezzler was captured in one of the buildings in the 1930's, after living there for weeks.

Pisgah was founded by a doctor, Finis E. Yoakum, from Larrica, Texas. His story is best told in his own words:

In 1894, I was practicing medicine in Denver, Colo. Riding on a Broadway car in that city, July 18th, on my way to organize a Class Leader's Association of the Methodist Church, I got off at 8 p.m., at the crossing of Cedar street. A drunken man was driving a horse furiously down the street at the time, and when I was fifteen feet away from the street car, the shaft of his buggy struck my body two inches to the left of my spine, breaking the seventh and eighth ribs, and hurling me forward. . . .

The doctors concluded I was dying. They thought the hemorrhage had taken place in the pleural cavity—which contains the heart and lungs. Their opinion was that a first hemorrhage had taken place when I was struck by

The main kitchen and dining room at Pisgah Grande had second-floor sleeping quarters for unmarried men. In the background, on the hill, is the old praying tower, where members of the Pisgah community took turns in praying to God around the clock. (Photograph by Paul Kagan)

the shaft of the buggy, and now a second hemorrhage had set in. They decided that the only thing that could be done was to cut out a part of the seventh rib. That was done, seven or eight Doctors being present, the chief surgeon operating. Two gallons of blood was let. After the operation was over, the surgeon cleaned his instruments, remarking to my wife: "The Doctor is dead;" and left the house.

Yoakum lay on his sickbed, barely alive, for several months and then, while still quite ill and against the advice of his friends and family, went to a place called the Christian Alliance, in Los Angeles, where they prayed for the sick:

Brother W. C. Stevens asked me my desire. I said, "I come to be healed in Jesus' name." After a few words of exhortation, they anointed me, laid their hands on me and prayed, claiming the fulfillment of the promise recorded in James 5:15, "The prayer of faith shall save the sick, and the Lord shall raise him up." My pain was more than I could endure—every joint seemed to be pulling asunder, every bone breaking. I told them I must go home.

Two brethren helped me downstairs. I suffered greater pain than I had known since I was first stricken. At the foot of the stairway, there is a flag-stone three inches above the pavement and as the brethren let go of me, I stepped upon the flagstone with my right foot, with my left foot toward the street below. Somewhere between the flagstone and the pavement—as already said, only three inches below—the Lord made me a free man! He delivered me from the power of the devil; the prayer of faith did save the sick, the Lord did raise me up.

The next morning, Yoakum was asked if he wished to have a surgeon remove the pus from his body:

Quickly I looked up and said: "I have taken Jesus as my Physician, and I now take Him as my Surgeon." Immediately there was a gurgling sound, and the pus came out through my bronchial tubes, filling a vessel, and scenting the house with a foul odor of rotten eggs, so that nobody could stay in the room.[1]

Healed, Yoakum went to the top of Mount Pisgah in the Arroyo Seco, threw his money on the ground, and dedicated himself to the work of the Lord. He then took to the back streets of Los Angeles, preaching the gospel of Christ to winos, cripples, and criminals, and many followed him. On Monday mornings he would go down to the jail when the drunks were let out and bring them to the Pisgah Home, which he had founded. "He'd give them a drink of water, and he'd pray for them, and, well, that would be the end

of it. They wouldn't drink no more."[2] He also had great success at a house of ill fame:

Around the table was all these prostitutes, family style. He sat down, and he talked to them, and he prayed, and when he left, the whole building got converted, and they shut the place down, and, of course, in shape like that they needed some place to take them, so he put them up in his house.[3]

His story became known, and donations to continue his work came from many places, some very far from Los Angeles. After a decade Dr. Yoakum's work encompassed Pisgah Home, "for the poor, especially the drunkard and down-and-out," Pisgah Ark, "for rescued women and girls, the cast-outs of society," Pisgah Store, "for the common people where the poor are supplied with what they need without money," and Pisgah Gardens (in the San Fernando Valley), "where consumptives and other sick folk are encouraged to trust the Lord for healing."[4] Yoakum said God could cure anything from cancer to lunacy through faith:

A woman was brought in a wheel chair to be healed. . . . Brother Yoakum left the platform to anoint this sister and commanded her in the name of Jesus to arise and walk. . . . She left her chair and walked away as she was commanded and when Brother Yoakum sat down a glory more than earthly over-spread his face as another triumph was scored for his Lord.[5]

Discarded crutches and canes were hung on the wall of the tabernacle of Pisgah Home, and written testimonials were often printed in the *Pisgah Journal*, many concerning the blessed handkerchiefs that Pisgah workers had prayed over and then mailed all over the world:

I was healed of cancer on my arm; I put the handkerchief on that night, and it was healed, and I was healed of rheumatism and many other things, and I do thank the Lord.

I had falling of the womb for twenty-seven years and was an agonizing sufferer, but after applying the handkerchief, I am now healed. I feel more thankful to God than words can express.

I had more physical ailments than usually fall to the lot of man. The first was a cough of over thirty years standing, with heavy expectorations. A leakage of the aortic valve of the heart, floating kidney, asthma, curved spine and dropsy of the limbs. I was led to California to find God and He is all I need.[6]

The inside of the old community kitchen at Pisgah Grande, unused for over forty years. (Photograph by Paul Kagan)

PISGAH HOME

A home for the poor, especially the drunkard and down-and-out, where the blood of Jesus Christ is daily exalted as the remedy for sin and sickness.

PISGAH ARK

A home for rescued women and girls, the cast-outs of society, where they are brought to a saving knowledge of the Lord Jesus Christ.

PISGAH GARDENS

Where consumptives and other sick folk are encouraged to trust the Lord for healing, and where quantities of fruit and vegetables are produced for the poor.

PISGAH FREE STORE

A common store for the common people where the poor are supplied with what they need without money and without price.

PISGAH HOME FOR NAMELESS CHILDREN

A home where cast-out children are brought up in the nurture and admonition of the Lord.

PISGAH JOURNAL

A free magazine telling how graciously God is working in the earth today.

ALL THINGS IN COMMON

The back cover of *Pisgah Home Songs*, listing the various facilities Yoakum operated for the downtrodden.

In 1914 Dr. Yoakum envisioned building a city to be called Pisgah Grande. He paid fifty thousand dollars for a 3,200-acre cattle ranch in the Santa Susana Mountains, on the Los Angeles County–Ventura County border. The land was isolated, fed by bountiful springs, and appeared to be an ideal spot to consecrate a city to God. Led by Father Yoakum, his followers went to work, the hills ringing with the Pisgah greeting of "Peace be unto thee."

The first oven was made of rocks piled together, and the biscuits were baked on pieces of sheet-iron while other pieces on which live coals had been placed were put over them that they might be baked through. Sister Nelle washed the Brothers' clothes in the mineral water of the creek with only the rocks of the creek to serve as a wash board; they slept on the ground in the rain.[7]

They prayed for the skills necessary to build a city and in fact became bricklayers and carpenters:

Clay suitable for brick was found with the necessary sand, and very shortly a crude brick yard was running, and they were turning out hundreds of bricks a day. One brother was put in charge of the brick making who knew absolutely nothing about the work and realizing this he went to the Matron, and holding out his hands, asked her to pray that the Lord would take them and teach them how to make bricks. Going back to the pit, he turned out 3600 brick that first day, the most that has ever been turned out in one day. The brick kiln was soon put up, and after some delays they were able to turn out 50,000 brick at one time.[8]

The property also contained sandstone, ready to be cut into blocks for building, and the natural materials necessary for making mortar. Soon a mission headquarters, a school, a dining hall, a post office, and residential houses were built. In addition, a new road from Pisgah to Chatsworth, the nearest town, was built through the canyon with pick and shovel, since the old road was too rough and difficult to travel.

More members arrived. There was a man who had been kicked in the head by a mule; his brain had been damaged in such a way that he walked and talked backwards. He was strong, though, and able to haul two huge water cans up the hill backward. There were also the prosperous and knowledgeable, who offered their various talents to the community. Those who understood engineering transformed the colony's springs into fountains that were channeled into an elaborate system of irrigation ditches. The crops included such traditionally biblical foods as melons and olives. Pisgah goats supplied milk; Pisgah bees supplied honey. The colonists used no eggs, meat, coffee,

"Wagon loaded with melons and fruit for the poor. Two pumpkins, weighing over 125 pounds each, just brought from gardens by Brother Cheek, Manager. Brother Karl Wittman loading his auto with tomatoes for the poor in the city. Mother Lawrence of Portland, Oregon, 'Pisgah Home,' sitting by a load of canteloupes. Standing on right of Brother Yoakum is a brother sent to us a few months ago from an insane asylum in a distant state, who has been healed by the blessed Christ. You will see two cases containing five-gallon cans of tomatoes." (Courtesy of H. J. Smith)

Founded in 1914, Pisgah Grande was a city consecrated to God. (Courtesy of H. J. Smith)

This cement mixer was made in 1893 and was used to mix the mortar for the Pisgah Grande buildings. Now it lies deserted, rusting in a meadow. (Photograph by Paul Kagan)

Pisgah Mill produced firewood for the poor and lumber for various Pisgah uses. The mill was located in the San Fernando Valley. (Courtesy of H. J. Smith)

tea, alcohol, or tobacco. Their simple needs were abundantly filled at Pisgah, with enough time left over to provide for beauty—every path was bordered with hundreds of bright flowers.

A never-ending vigil was kept in the prayer tower, which was on top of a hill overlooking the colony and had windows facing all four directions. The colony's members prayed in shifts for twenty-four hours a day.

Daily life at Pisgah Grande is best described in the words of an old man who lived there when he was young:

For breakfast we had a great big bowl of oatmeal mush with a big square of butter and real milk on it and two or three spoons of sorghum and fruit, stewed apricots, or something like that. And boy, as a kid I thought, boy, I'm living like a king! That's food! And then after that we would go out and feed the stock, or some of us would herd the cattle. . . . In the fall of the year I remember I stripped sorghum. They let the sorghum grow up, and then they stripped it with a stick and knocked the leaves off, and then they cut it, and us kids would feed these stalks through a mill with three rollers. The juice came out sort of milky like. Up on the hill we had a big cement trough, and with fire under it, the juice became a syrup which they would boil down and skim and put in cans. Yeah, that's what we had for sweetening. . . . On Sundays we had milking the cows in the morning and evening, feeding the stock; the rest of the time as I remember would be church services.[9]

Most of the work was under the direction of James Cheek, who had been converted in 1911: "I was dying with consumption. Through the prayers of Brother Yoakum I was healed of catarrh, bowel trouble, influenza, and also of unbelief." In his autobiography Cheek recounted the story of Pisgah Grande's best-known resident—Billy Stiles, the youngest member of the Jesse James gang:

He had been saved and was then a very consecrated man and liked to talk about what the Lord had done for

James Cheek was married at Pisgah Home in the 1920's. (Courtesy of the Huntington Library)

him. We enjoyed hearing him talk. He sometimes talked about the life of the gang. He described the Blue Cut train robbery and the Coffeyville, Kansas bank robbery. . . . He said they would sometimes join the posse which was looking for them and not be discovered. . . .

Also Billy told about the night he was converted. He with other of the gang had made preparation to rob a train out of Los Angeles and, to get off the street and out of sight, he went into the Union Rescue Mission on Main Street. . . . He was asked to go to the altar, and, being in a mood not to care what he did, he responded to the call. Somehow the spirit of God got hold of him that night and he was converted. He then went to the gang and told them about his conversion. . . . Jesse James would go to church with his wife, posting some of the gang as guards around the church.[10]

While Pisgah Grande took form, the other Yoakum institutions in Los Angeles also prospered, but they also began to draw criticism, largely over the issue of money. It was alleged that Dr. Yoakum became rich on the donations to Pisgah and lived with his wife in luxury yet at the same time failed to provide as well as he could for the inmates of his institutions. An unpublished manuscript in the library of the Los Angeles *Times* mentions the assumption that feeding Pisgah's dependents was very costly:

Under normal conditions this would be true but the assumption loses much of its force when one learns of the transcendant virtue of Pisgah Stew, the pièce de résistance of all Yoakum institutions.

Pisgah Stew . . . what nauseating nightmares are given free rein; what abdominal tortures recalled; what conception of man's damnable ingenuity brought to realization, with thought of that famous or infamous concoction of warm water, kidney beans, and uncooked cabbage. . . . This is the menu three hundred and sixty-five days in each year. . . .

Understanding that vegetables are raised in the gardens; that meat is utterly lacking; that bread for the most part is donated and that the inmates do all the work, one is led to the conclusion that the cost of maintenance is not a severe strain on Dr. Yoakum, who handles the finances. It must not be understood that the restrictions as to food extend to Dr. Yoakum and his family. Chicken and choice viands are on the table daily if one may credit the statements of the Yoakum servants.

The manuscript contains additional, perhaps exaggerated, claims. The mysterious author, who signed himself only H.C.D., claimed that although Yoakum did provide at least Pisgah Stew for "flotsam and jetsam upon the sea of life," harmless bums who had nothing better to eat, he also harbored criminals. According to H.C.D., large numbers of Los Angeles

Yoakum and the faithful in a formal group portrait (ca. 1915). (Courtesy of H. J. Smith)

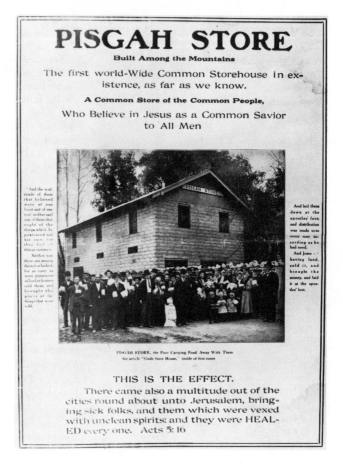

PISGAH STORE

Built Among the Mountains

The first world-Wide Common Storehouse in existence, as far as we know.

A Common Store of the Common People,

Who Believe in Jesus as a Common Savior to All Men

PISGAH STORE, the Poor Carrying Food Away With Them
See article "God's Store House," inside of first cover

THIS IS THE EFFECT.

There came also a multitude out of the cities round about unto Jerusalem, bringing sick folks, and them which were vexed with unclean spirits: and they were HEALED every one. Acts 5: 16

The first "free store" in California, built ca. 1909. (Courtesy of H. J. Smith)

thieves and con men admitted that they "cover at ol' Doc Yoakum's" when the heat is on.

Although H.C.D. did not criticize Pisgah for feeding "lazy worthless bums and drunkards," he was unhappy that no effort was made "to induce these derelicts to straighten up; to go out in the world, secure work and make something of themselves. . . . On the contrary every inducement is offered to get them to renounce the normal life and to become permanent inmates of Pisgah." H.C.D. concluded that Father Yoakum was more or less a man of the devil who preyed on the fanatical devotion of his followers, which he won through the force of his peculiar personality and turned into a life of luxury for himself. That his followers were indeed devoted is doubtless. When questioned on the prosperity of the Yoakums, Sister Nell, the first in command at Pisgah Home, replied: "The Lord has wonderfully blessed Father and Mother Yoakum in the possession of worldly goods. . . . In Pisgah Home we witness many miracles."

This devotion can also be measured by the fact that the Yoakums' Los Angeles residence was built by Pisgah workers with no pay whatsoever. When construction began, Dr. Yoakum was away and Mrs. Yoakum gave the workers $1.50 a day plus lunch, which the Father proclaimed "a waste of the Lord's money" and stopped on his return.

According to H.C.D., Yoakum's revenue came from contributions at the tabernacle services ($400–$450 a week from people "wrought up" by the quality of the preaching), a 50 percent cut from the pay of the few residents of Pisgah Home who held jobs outside, and an active mail-order business in blessed handkerchiefs at $5 apiece. H.C.D. estimated Dr. Yoakum's income at $500,000 a year.

H.C.D.'s story is supported by a memorandum dated June 25, 1918, in the files of the Los Angeles *Times*, concerning a Mr. Denison—physician, scientist, and inventor—who went to Pisgah Home, apparently with the idea of helping Dr. Yoakum make

SCENES AT PISGAH GRANDE

Upper Left—Brother Yoakum driving "Beauty." Sister Nina and School Children. Upper Right—Brother Yoakum, Sister Lillian, Sister Dixon, Brother Karl Wittman. Center—Watch Tower on mountain overlooking Main Camp. Lower Left—The Family Group. Lower Right—Sister Nina, Brother Yoakum, Sister Dixon.

Devoted to the Material Welfare, Bodily Healing, Moral Uplift and Spiritual Life of the Stricken in Body, Victim of Drink, Outcast, Cripple, Hungry, Friendless and

WHOSOEVER IS IN NEED OF THE WATERS OF LIFE

PUBLISHED AT PISGAH GRANDE   LOS ANGELES COUNTY, CALIFORNIA

Pisgah, cheaply produced, was a forerunner of the tracts and testimonials handed out by Pentecostal Christians on street corners today. (Courtesy of H. J. Smith)

the home industrialized and self-supporting. Denison left after four weeks, calling Pisgah a "hypocritical, money-making scheme." He said Dr. Yoakum bragged about the properties he acquired for Pisgah enterprises and "used the poor and afflicted simply as a means to get donations from all over the country." Denison felt that an investigation would reveal a misuse of the mail for obtaining money under false pretenses. He further claimed that Dr. Yoakum exercised absolute control over the people at Pisgah, who obeyed every command, could not even talk to one another without his permission, and were fed "vile and unnourishing" foods, consisting mostly of "soup and stale bread and unmarketable potatoes." Denison left Pisgah without intending to do anything about what he had discovered there, but he received a letter from an old crippled woman, a member of the community, imploring him to help change conditions, as she could do nothing from the inside. Therefore, although he did not wish to have his statements published, he was

communicating with the *Times,* hoping that the paper would cooperate with the city in a formal investigation. (The Reverend H. J. Smith, of the Christ Faith Mission–Pisgah movement, correctly pointed out to the author that the refusal of the Los Angeles *Times* to print the criticisms of H.C.D. and Mr. Denison may have indicated a reluctance of the paper's editors to print material that they deemed unsubstantiated.)

Accusations and rumors notwithstanding, the *Times* apparently felt the criticisms to be highly questionable, and nothing was done. Most of the press coverage Pisgah received in the next two years simply acknowledged the various charitable activities of Dr. Yoakum. Around the same time as the Denison memorandum, Pisgah Home announced a mass baptism and foot-washing ceremony prior to a nationwide tour by Dr. Yoakum. (This was not the first such tour. Dr. Yoakum had made one in 1914 and attempted to start a Pisgah movement in San Francisco, his first stop.) The announcement included an accounting of past

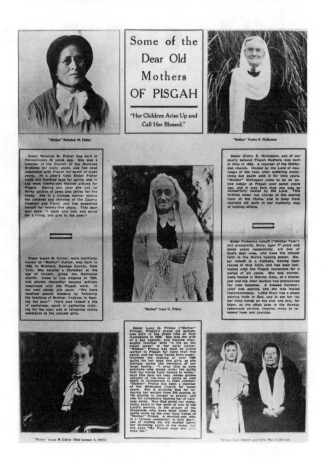

"Some of the Dear Old Mothers OF PISGAH" superintended various activities such as quilt-making, sewing, and the care of the sick and needy. Several of the mothers themselves were miraculously cured of afflictions through the use of blessed handkerchiefs and the laying on of hands. (Courtesy of H. J. Smith)

achievements: Pisgah had furnished more than 300,000 free meals and more than 100,000 free lodgings annually, "with free baths and clean wearing apparel to the lodgers." These statements were carried without comment, or sometimes with favorable comment, by much of the local press, perhaps remembering Dr. Yoakum's grand gesture several years earlier, when he had invited two thousand of the poor and unfortunate to his daughter's wedding, citing the Bible as precedent: "When thou makest a dinner or a supper, call not thy friends, nor thy bretheren, neither thy kinsmen, nor any rich neighbors, but the poor, the maimed, the lame, the blind."

Dr. Yoakum maintained a consistent policy of praying for those who were blind enough to criticize him and his work, and perhaps his prayers were answered, for trouble never seriously threatened Pisgah until the doctor's death in August, 1920. Pisgah, like so many other community endeavors, centered its life around one man, and when that pivotal presence was gone,

everything else began to fail. "They had lost their strong leadership, and each one who was left behind felt that it should be done this way, or it should be done that way. Well, in the course of a few years everybody had a chance to do with it as they thought best, but the strong leadership was lacking; Dr. Yoakum's leadership wasn't there. And he was the man with the vision."[11]

Dr. Yoakum's sons, Charles and Finis, who inherited the property, were not in sympathy with their father's work. Within a few months of his death Pisgah Home was under investigation by a Los Angeles County grand jury, a procedure instigated by a report from a county health officer which condemned the sanitary facilities.

At Pisgah Grande the colonists began to depart, until only a few of the very old, with no place else to call home, were left. They spent much of their time attending to the cemetery, which had been chosen for the special quality of its soil, which was expected

Today, furniture decays slowly on the forgotten patio of a Pisgah Grande home. (Photograph by Paul Kagan)

This is the last photograph taken of Pisgah's founder, often referred to as Daddy Yoakum, before his death in August, 1920. (Courtesy of H. J. Smith)

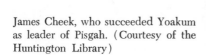

James Cheek, who succeeded Yoakum as leader of Pisgah. (Courtesy of the Huntington Library)

Rev. H. J. Smith runs the Christ Faith Mission in Los Angeles in the same quarters once occupied by the Pisgah Home. (Photograph by Paul Kagan)

to petrify the bodies against decay. The graves were kept covered with flowers until there were no flowers left. Finally, Charles and Finis allowed the county authorities to drive the old people out. "They intended to live there, you know, the rest of their days. But when the thing sort of deteriorated, they really evicted these people. And believe it or not, the judgment of God came upon a lot of those people. They became involved in all kinds of things themselves, and some of them went into prison."[12]

Deserted and spooky, Pisgah Grande has a ghost story attached to it now. Several people have claimed to have seen a steady white light the size and shape of a square hatbox swooping around in the Pisgah trees.

The Pisgah movement remained in Los Angeles for several years. (In 1925 it appealed to the *Times* to publicize its need for donations, but after checking its files and making an inquiry to the Social Service Commission, the *Times* refused.) Pisgah then moved its headquarters to the San Bernardino Mountains and later to Pikeville, Tennessee, where it still survives.

James Cheek became the editor and publisher of the *Herald of Hope,* an evangelical magazine. In 1952 he wrote to Professor Robert V. Hine, then doing research on California communities: "In regard to the scandal which was set afloat, it sounds strange to most of the people who knew Dr. Yoakum best . . . considering the thousands of lives which were transformed in various ways, spiritually and physically."

In 1972 the Pisgah movement came back to its original home in Los Angeles and combined its publications and religious activities with the Christ Faith Mission, which had taken over the publication of the *Herald of Hope* after Cheek's death in 1954. The Christ Faith Mission had operated out of the old Pisgah property in Los Angeles since 1939, still calling its buildings "Pisgah." The property had been sold after Yoakum's death but came back into Christian hands when a woman called Mother Green was told by the Lord to buy it and resurrect its tradition. Christ Faith Mission is today an active, proselytizing, hardcore Jesus movement, and it venerates the memory of Dr. Yoakum.

The raw, unfinished woodwork and the unimproved buildings have brought the present Pisgah Home to task by the Los Angeles building-code authorities. A program of renovation has begun. (Photograph by Paul Kagan)

Ornate signs and antiquated light fixtures from the original Pisgah enterprises still provide inspiration to the members of the Christ Faith Mission. This sign might have been made at Pisgah Grande around 1915. (Photograph by Paul Kagan)

Pisgah Grande today is a ghost town. Pictured here are the post office (far left), the dining room and men's dormitory (center left), the kitchen (center right), and the administration office (upper center). (Photograph by Paul Kagan)

Zen students are greeted by this handmade sign at the Tassajara Zen Mountain Center after they traverse fourteen miles of a steep, winding dirt road in the Santa Lucia Mountains. (Photograph by Paul Kagan)

CHAPTER 9

Tassajara Zen Mountain Center

At times in our busy lives the teachings of Buddhism and even Zen practice may provide only a respite from our trivial and fond concerns. At Tassajara it is different. There is the physical beauty, the considerateness of its monks, its thoughtfully ordered life, the example of its teacher. Above all there is the quiet. Here Buddhism can be lived, and Zen practice seems the most natural thing in the world.
—Albert Stunkard, M.D.
Chairman, Department of Psychiatry
Stanford University[1]

Zen Buddhism in America conjures up different images for the casual reader. The recent profusion of Eastern cults, philosophies, and religions in Western society has tended to make the onlooker suspicious of the seemingly alien quality of the meditative postures of *zazen*, the forty-minute periods of sitting quietly twice daily (or, at Tassajara, five times daily). The practice of *zazen*, however, is just one aspect of the disciplined Zen Buddhist way. Now the whole of the Zen process is to be found in the California Zen Center. With its headquarters in San Francisco, where some sixty people live and work together, the center operates a traditional Zen monastery on 160 acres at the Tassajara hot springs in a wilderness area about a ninety-minute drive from Monterey.

To get to the monastery itself one must drive over fourteen miles of dirt road, up a perilous grade to a level of five thousand feet and then down at a steep angle into a beautiful valley. During the summer at the Tassajara Zen Mountain Center, or *Zenshinji* (Zen mind-heart temple), the visitor is greeted by the gatekeeper. It is his job to register the summer guests coming to the hot springs and to offer to new Zen students a chance to participate fully in the strenuous Zen work program.

Inside the gate one finds industrious activity: Men and women work together cutting firebreaks, washing clothes, and cooking and quietly attending to other chores. In the spring and summer after Tassajara was bought by the California Zen Center in 1967, members of the community did over fifty thousand dollars' worth of clean-up, repairs, and gardening. The sense of the physical work and the formal spiritual practice, however, were adopted to help the Zen devotee find his own inner work, free of all the forms and traditions with which he was engaged on the outside. "This sense of how Buddhism should exist in America was in sharp focus during the [first] practice period when we were faced over and over again with details like: Do we wear robes or not, and what kind of robes? Shall this ceremony be simplified? How? Shall it be in English? Should we chant in English or Japanese?"[2] More and more an "American" Zen Buddhism was sought after, so that rituals such as bowing would be more than just the outer form. The problem of communicating the meaning of the practices and of adapting them to an American form without losing their deeper sense was ultimately the responsibility of the teacher and founder of the California Zen Center, Shunryu Suzuki, who came to California in 1958 from Japan, where he had been a respected Zen master, the son of another Zen master.

The fascinating history of Tassajara, with its 1870 buildings that saw use as barbershops, bars, and hotels, really starts with the accounts of the Pacific Coast Indian tribes, who told of their reverence for the curative powers of the hot springs. The story was developed in an early issue of *Wind Bell,* the California Zen Center's excellent magazine:

In 1843, a hunter hiking up the Carmel Valley met a party of Indians on their way into the mountains. Their leader, who spoke Spanish well and so must have been a Mission Indian, told the hunter that they were going to the hot springs to cure a skin disease which had broken out among them. They planned to "build a seat hut of mud and branches over the place where the hot water flowed from the ground [the site of the present-day vapor rooms] and then remain there until they got so weak the medicine man would have to carry them out. After that they would scrape their bodies with the ribs of deer or some other wild animal."

When the Indians stopped using the springs is not known, but by 1868 Frank Rust had opened a camp there, and by the early 1870's "Doc" Chambers and "Rocky" Beasly were hunting out of the caves five miles upstream. These caves had been inhabited for at least a thousand years by Indians, who had left white prints of their hands on the walls. Often the springs were occupied by several tribes at once, perhaps by the Costanoans of Monterey and Soledad who could have come down the Church Creek from the Caves, and the Salinans from the Jolon/San Antonio Mission area who could have come upstream from the Arroyo Seco. There was reputedly so much game at the springs that there was never much quarreling among the tribes. When they did fight elsewhere—which was seldom—the moment the first person on either side fell, everyone retreated.

Because the way into the springs was so inaccessible,

Shunryu Suzuki founded Tassajara, the first Zen monastery in the United States. An excellent book on Zen practice, *Zen Mind, Beginner's Mind,* is based on his talks to his students. (Photograph by Paul Kagan, 1967)

This is a *shuso* (head monk) ceremony during an intensive training period at Tassajara. The teacher is
Tatsugami-roshi, in the hooded robe. Everyone asks a
question of the *shuso* during the ceremony. (Courtesy of
the Zen Center)

particularly to those who sought to be cured by them, the
squatters who succeeded Frank Rust after he vacated his
camp the winter of '69 usually stayed less than a year,
despite the still great quantities of game, "from quail to
grizzly bear which abounded there." "Rocky" Beasly
claimed to have killed 132 such bear.

The first settler with entrepreneuring aspirations was
Jack Borden and the name he gave the springs was Tassajara, i.e., a place where meat is dried and jerked, even
though meat had most likely never been cured there. Until
then the springs had been called Aqua Caliente (Hot
Water), a name the Spaniards had given to all the hot
springs in California.[3]

At the time the land for the Tassajara Zen Mountain
Center was selected, in 1966, the followers of Suzuki-
roshi (*roshi* means "master") in San Francisco numbered over a hundred. The small group shouldered
a debt of $300,000 for the land and buildings, but by
the spring of 1972 the last of the $20,000 mortgage
payments had been made.

Money was raised with the help of hundreds of
supporters throughout the country. Among them were
notable literary and artistic figures, such as novelist
Herbert Gold, who gave the center his Jaguar sedan
in 1967. It was traded for a new six-ton Dodge platform truck. In the early days of the rock dances at
the Avalon and Fillmore auditoriums in San Francisco,
a "Zenefit" was given to help the center. Gary Snyder,
Alan Watts, and other Zen-men were active (and
still are) in helping the mountain community.

As work on the Tassajara grounds progressed, the
members of the community did as much as possible
to leave undisturbed the natural balance of the Tassajara wilderness environment, feeling that there was
"something elemental about the valley with its waterfalls at both ends, its natural hot springs, clear streams,

Students working on the foundation of the new kitchen at Tassajara in 1967. (Courtesy of the Zen Center)

and old trees and buildings."[4] The diet needed to supply the energy for the work to be done was more than the spartan fare one might expect, although it was not unnecessarily indulgent. The care and attentiveness that went into the baking of bread was so exceptional that the best-selling *Tassajara Bread Book* has been one result. After experimenting with Oriental and American diets, "the final diet was chosen for its spiritual and nutritious qualities rather than its nationalistic. The food was vegetarian, but because of the great amount of outside work that was done, and because of the need to balance the transition from the previous diet of the students to the new monastery diet, such protein staples as eggs and cheese were added to the diet."[5]

Much of the food comes from Tassajara's own gardens:

We try to rotate crops and now grow the same thing twice on the same land. Each season we leave about half the land fallow, growing barley and vetch as cover crops on it. When planting time nears we spread chicken manure over the grass and turn it all under. Add some bone meal, some phosphorus, and as much compost as we can. Plant a month later. Five years of this might give us some good garden soil. A nursery man in Monterey said, when we

began 3 years ago, "You can't grow a garden up there. The winter rains come through that valley and wash out all the good soil and the creek takes it down to Salinas and *that's* where you grow vegetables." The creek outside my window runs brown this rainy February day. He's right. But we're trying anyway. We've had fresh vegetables from the garden every day this year.[6]

One member of the Zen community was so involved in the work and administration of the kitchen that he wrote about kitchen rules:

A dull knife will not cut,
Nor a cracked bowl hold water.
Putting your mind and body in order,
How useful everything becomes.

    Looking for the knife
    Which is not there—
    How hard to find.

Washing rice, kneading bread,
Chopping carrots, peeling oranges,
Slicing pickles, saving crumbs,
No time for living, no time to die.[7]

Inseparable from the intensive physical work at Tassajara is the rigorous spiritual discipline. All those active in the community rise at 3:40 A.M. and then sit for two forty-minute periods of *zazen* at 4:00 A.M. The schedule then calls for service, breakfast, a study period, a 2½-hour work period, midday *zazen*, lunch, a rest period, a 3-hour work period, bath time, service, supper, lecture, and one or two more periods of *zazen* before bed at 9:45 P.M. Some of these activities are heralded by the hitting of wood sounding-boards, ceremonial instruments originated in China over a thousand years ago. The sounds not only serve to inform the members of the Tassajara community of a scheduled event but also convey an impressive and symbolic dignity.

The students who maintain the monastery come from all over the United States and from some other countries as well. They grow their food, attend to the hot-springs guest facilities in the summer, and develop their spiritual practice at Tassajara. Most are between the ages of eighteen and thirty-five, but some are as old as seventy. Their occupations range from kindergarten teacher to gold miner. The Zen community at Tassajara has included college professors, psychiatrists, Jungian analysts, importers, bookstore owners, technical writers, housewives, and even a naval commander.

Two of Tassajara's members were described in *The Village Voice* in 1967:

Peter Schneider, Tassajara's Director, is one of the most articulate of the pioneering group. An affable, good-looking man in his late 20's, he has several years of graduate school behind him as well as desultory teaching of English and math. Throughout local Zendom he is known as the

Suzuki-roshi (right) and one of his oldest students working in the *roshi's* garden. (Photograph by Robert S. Boni, courtesy of the Zen Center)

From left to right, Richard Baker, Suzuki-roshi, and Chino-sensei practicing *zazen* at Tassajara. (Courtesy of the Zen Center)

During *zazen* the *junko* corrects the students' sitting posture when necessary. This is done by striking the student with a stick, after which the *junko* is silently thanked with a bow. Chino-sensei is the *junko* here. (Courtesy of the Zen Center)

Students during *kinhin* (walking meditation). (Photograph by Paul Kagan)

man who sat zazen alone for two years—something of a solo flight record, considering one usually sits with others, or with priestly guidance. . . . Then along comes a young man named Dan [Welch]. He offers quite a contrast to the others. Both he and his attractive wife dress in such rural roughness—he in faded overalls, she in long, plain dresses—they seem to be walking right off the remotest of west Kansas farms. Both have a farmland kind of taciturnity too. Yet Dan wears the flowing, near shoulder-length hair that would never blossom atop any Kansas farmer. He's also spent two years in a Japanese monastery, and has gone farther with meditation than many of his fellow Tassajarans.[8]

Unlike Japanese monasteries, Tassajara admits both men and women, including married couples. During several summers at Tassajara, a school for young children has been tried. *Wind Bell* described the 1969 school program:

Is Tassajara a monastery, and if so, how can we practice a monastic life with children underfoot? Or, is Tassajara an intentional practice community, and if so, why can't we have marriages and children here? We had decided early on that, as a community, there should be room for married couples at Tassajara. Children seemed another problem entirely, complicated by the lack of facilities—schools or nurseries—and by the worry that they would disrupt the monastic atmosphere and distract their mothers and fathers from the communal practice.

The children came themselves and showed us what to do: feed them regularly on the porch behind the zendo, but balance the brown rice and miso soup with pancakes and eggs occasionally. Encourage them to come inside for services and zazen and lectures if they wanted to, and between times, let them run around and play and generally figure out how to take care of themselves in this new and wild mountain canyon world. This worked out well. Their ages were spread enough so that there were always older children to catch the younger ones when they were on the verge of directly investigating the true nature of rattle-

Ringing the *densho* bell for service at Tassajara.
(Photograph by Paul Kagan)

A meeting in the early days of Tassajara to discuss the problems in Zen practice and life at Tassajara. (Photograph by Robert S. Boni, courtesy of the Zen Center)

Lunch preparation in the Tassajara kitchen during the fall of 1973. Two best-selling books have resulted from the kitchen techniques at Tassajara, *The Tassajara Bread Book* (1970) and *Tassajara Cooking* (1973), both by Edward Espe Brown. (Photograph by Robert S. Boni, courtesy of the Zen Center)

Student Dan Welch working on the meditation hall at Tassajara. (Photograph by Tim Buckley, courtesy of the Zen Center)

A student at Tassajara learns how to repair a *geta,* a flat wooden shoe, from Chino-sensei, who was the teacher at Tassajara during 1968. (Photograph by Minoru Aoki, courtesy of the Zen Center)

snakes and high cliffs; enough younger children to keep the older ones from becoming overbearing, enough time in between zendo and work schedules for parents to be with their children, and more than enough resilience among the single Zen students to absorb the children into the community. In fact, almost everyone seemed pleased with this new aspect of life at Tassajara.[9]

When Suzuki-roshi died in 1972, the Zen tradition in California passed entirely into American hands. Richard Baker, a long-time disciple, became the *roshi* of the California Zen Center. Baker-roshi takes note of the social limitations and implications of Zen practice:

Zazen doesn't help everybody. Sometimes emotionally disturbed people are attracted to Zen practice or alternative ways of life, and Zen Center in San Francisco has developed ways based on the traditional Buddhist "weeding-out" practices of China and Japan of limiting the participation of such persons to the degree of participation which helps them. This weeding-out process is begun long before such persons would enter the more austere and strict Buddhist life and Zen practice at Tassajara. *Tangaryo*—the five or more days of uninterrupted sitting required for entrance into the traditional Zen monastery—is a condensed form of this weeding-out practice.

In 1972, to balance the mountain and city centers, the California Zen Center acquired a large farm in Marin County, near San Francisco. The Zen students see this as completing the basic form of a Zen center: a city *zendo* (meditation hall) and study center, a traditional Zen monastery in the mountains (Tassajara), a farm (the new Green Gulch Farm in Marin County), and a necessary workable limitation of two hundred students.

A Zen monastery is not meant to be so isolated a community that the interdependence of man upon man is forgotten, so the average student lives at the isolated Tassajara community for only a while—

Children at Tassajara making *rakusu* (Buddha's robe). (Courtesy of the Zen Center)

usually two to three years. Meanwhile, the larger practical religious communities of the city and farm centers are directly a part of ordinary American society. In this way, Tassajara comes closer to the society around it than many of the experiments that were aimed at founding a "new world." The individual Zen community is seen as only a part of the Zen practice that goes on in other Zen communities all over the United States, and if Tassajara is only a part, it is precisely in this part that the whole Zen process can be seen. Tassajara effectively raises the idea of a world-within-worlds; it is itself a whole and functioning little community, well aware of its dependence on the bigger community around it, and also cognizant of society's need for such monastic retreats to exist.

The real opportunity for the California Zen Center to develop the relationships between Zen practice and society came about through the acquisition of Green Gulch Farm, with its easy access to the city and the surrounding community. In 1974 Zen students wrote:

Zen Center is trying to find out what the bases of living and working together are: what are the bases of the household, the nuclear family, the priorities of the household of possessions and attachments, the diverse community and service to others, and Zen practice which moves and is a giving up of attachments; and what are the bases of personality and attachments (ignorance, greed, hate, delu-

An early *Wind Bell* jokingly captioned this as "Suzuki-roshi inspecting Tassajara's first rice crop." (Photograph by Clarke Mason, courtesy of the Zen Center)

Suzuki-roshi's widow, usually called Okusan, at Tassajara in 1973. She is continuing her work with the center at present. (Photograph by Paul Kagan)

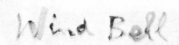

PUBLICATION OF ZEN CENTER   VOLUME XII, 1973

Wind Bell is published irregularly by the
Zen Center.

sion) which when given up make a joyful and realized
life possible.

During the summer the Tassajara students are
brought into a relationship with the outside world by
the many visitors to the historic Tassajara hot springs.
Members of the Tassajara community care for and
feed the guests for a very reasonable fifteen dollars
a night. The visitors are brought in contact not only
with the physical comfort of the soothing hot springs
but also with the vital force of Zen Buddhism as practiced at Tassajara. When long-time summer visitors
to the hot springs were concerned that Tassajara might
be closed to them when the Zen Mountain Center took
over the land,

they were assured that this was not the case, that we felt
a commitment to them, since land, particularly this historical California hot springs of such great beauty, should
be open as much as possible to those who want to use it
and have been using it for years. It is also important

San Francisco Zen Center, located at 300 Page Street, was purchased in November, 1969. (Courtesy of the Zen Center)

Green Gulch Farm in Marin County before its acquisition by the Zen Center in 1972. (Courtesy of the Zen Center)

Richard Baker-roshi, who succeeded Suzuki-roshi as the head of the Zen Center in 1972. (Courtesy of the Zen Center)

Alan Chadwick, an expert gardener, teaching Zen students and his own apprentices the principles of gardening and soil conservation at Green Gulch Farm. This program lasted a year and helped produce the present gardens at Green Gulch. (Courtesy of the Zen Center)

The first Green Gulch *sesshin* (a week-long intensive practice period). The old barn had been converted into a new *zendo*. Students ate and slept where they sat during the *sesshin* in October of 1973. (Courtesy of the Zen Center)

that Zen Mountain Center not be isolated from the communities around it, as a monastery is a place where students are trained so that they can go back into such communities.[10]

Tassajara remains closed to guests during most of the fall, winter, and spring months, when the roads are impassable. During this time intensive programs of spiritual discipline are carried out. The responsibility for guiding these activities and for teaching Zen at the California Zen Center has passed from Suzuki-roshi to Richard Baker. As the first American *roshi* of the center, Baker-roshi has a unique and heavy responsibility. Educated in the United States and Japan, Baker-roshi is now faced with the kind of problem that has always plagued spiritual communities: how to continue in such a way that a new generation of students receives a direct experience of Zen Buddhism comparable to the sense of Zen that he and his fellow students received from their teacher, Suzuki-roshi. The possible advantage that the Zen community has over nontraditional teachings like Theosophy and Fountaingrove's Brotherhood of the New Life is that the Zen community is grounded in an enduring tradition that does not derive its strength and sustenance solely from the fiery zeal of a leader like Katherine Tingley or Thomas Lake Harris.

When a community is based almost wholly on the energy and wisdom of its founder, it is bound to fail within a generation or two of the death of the leader. Zen Buddhism, however, has 2,500 years of background in the Orient. It may be that through the efforts of the older students of Suzuki-roshi and the diligent questioning of the new students of Zen, the California Zen Center will have an enduring future.

Conclusion

California has been aptly called the America of America. In the attraction it has held for the adventurous, the desperate, the bold and imaginative, it has in some measure preserved the old dream our founding fathers shared of a new land, a new community defined not only politically but also spiritually. It was only natural, therefore, that with the eventual complication and breakdown of the original spiritual ideals of the American community, these ideals in somewhat changed form moved west.

This is an important consideration if we wish to understand the difference between a contemporary American commune and the older European forms of communal organization—the monasteries, in particular. The commune is a *nation* on a tiny scale—at least that is its ideal. Unlike the traditional religious communities of European Christianity, the commune is a segment of this world and not a segment of heaven brought down to earth. If this distinction is forgotten, we are bound to make invidious comparisons between the often invented religiosity of the California communes and the more objective and immeasurably longer-lasting sacred traditions of the communities of the past. The commune, like America, starts as a *place* —an open space in which to experiment in living one's ideals. It is open-ended; it can go anywhere; there is faith in time. This is American, and it is intensely Californian, despite the proclamations of some com-

mune members about the imminent end of the world as we know it.

We may easily judge this faith as naiveté—faith that there is time, that one has one's freedom, that man is naturally good, and that it is the function of the earth to support this goodness—but something similar seems to be believed by most Americans. It is a set of assumptions about life that has been largely hidden from view by the development of a technology that now tends to govern man instead of serving him.

I look again at these photographs, at the windy desolation of ruins that are not beautiful as are the ruins of Europe. Time has been unkind to them, that same time in which the communities' founders had so much faith. The animals play freely under the rotting boards, and vegetation crawls over a table that once held a new scripture. What went wrong, and can we answer that without understanding what goes wrong in our own attempts to come together and live as free human beings? What are the forces that oppose this? Where is our naiveté?

Certainly one factor is the Californian expectation that great ideas and great trust in man is enough. The early Hindu cults that flourished in California stressed the divinity of human nature rather than the sin and guilt that is the substance of East Coast American-European Protestant Christianity. (The Quakers of Pennsylvania were one of several exceptions to this,

When Vedanta came to the United States at the end of the nineteenth century, introducing previously unfamiliar Eastern religious ideas to energetic and open Americans, it took a tenacious hold in California. Christopher Isherwood, Aldous Huxley, and Gerald Heard were among the many people who participated in Vedanta communities and religious activities. This is in the courtyard of Ananda Ashram, in Los Angeles County, which has remained relatively independent of the other Vedanta groups during its long stay in California. (Photograph by Paul Kagan)

however. They also sought for an inner contact with divinity, but their family structures and their habits of behavior still reflected the ancient patriarchal conception of family life.)

California offered the American dream, the land of gold, the growth of technical prowess, and comfort of life. People came to California and shed what George Santayana called the "genteel tradition." They kicked off their shoes, and the women took off their corsets. It is still happening, but now in the realm of constraining thoughts and feelings, cast off and thrown aside because they never were a real part of us anyway; we had always been afraid to let go of them. "See, I am liberated without them. Now I can live and work. There are no hang-ups in this new-found freedom."

Is this true, however? This is the core of the California dream, the weakness in its strength. The habits come back, the emotional structure of man is not so easily changed, and what was experienced as freedom and "togetherness" soon becomes only a memory or an ideal. Disillusion sets in and is tranquilized with drugs, a succession of gurus, or with ideas, even great religious ideas and programs. We are back full circle: America leads to America. California remains California whether it is a natural geographical area or a California of the mind, with its own great waterfalls, redwoods, deserts, and prairies. In rushing away from the artificiality of technological life, are we turning from the place where our real problems and history are reflected? The city may be a bad place; science may have no room for Atman and Brahman; but nothing can be changed until we see ourselves as we really are.

Are there ideas and a structure of community life through which we can see the fragments of ourselves as they really are, not as they should be? Ask any disillusioned commune member—he will say that he left because the old tensions, jealousies, and conflicts arrived at the new destination. Did he *see* them arrive? Did he watch the process by which the deeply engraved habits and fragmentations of man reasserted themselves? If so, perhaps he has begun to know himself—but if not, then the whole experience may

The Rosicrucians in California were another popular group for early-twentieth-century disillusioned Christians, who suspected that a richer meaning existed in religious teaching than that taught by the traditional churches. This is the main temple of the southern California Rosicrucians. They are independent of their wealthier brethren in San Jose, and their astrological publications are widely circulated in all countries. (Photograph by Paul Kagan)

The Lama Foundation is located in the mountains of New Mexico. Organized in 1967, the Lama commune emphasizes its experimental nature. A large number of people have participated in the hard physical work at Lama in the attempt to build a lasting community. (Photograph by Paul Kagan)

have been wasted. He says he worked hard, but he had no idea it would be necessary to depend upon the outside world so much—even for sustenance. It is an interconnected world, we reply to ourselves. Didn't he know that?

Have the Eastern religions attracting these people been formulated in ways that take into account the population explosion, the development of worldwide communications media, and the creaking financial structure of Western industrial society? Do any groups or individuals have a teaching comprehensive and suitable enough to meet both the spiritual and the technological needs of Western man?

The outside world has a tendency to look at members of communal groups in stereotyped ways. Direct contact with various communal experiments, however, creates an appreciation of the efforts and results of the individuals involved and reaffirms the promise that communal efforts hold for the future. An historic example of the fruits of communal endeavor is the role played by Theosophists and Vedantists in introducing ideas sacred in the East to Western culture. The early efforts of these groups helped to make accessible the wide body of Eastern religious writings that are attracting so much interest today.

We know so little about the source of new ideas and how they enter a society. Unfamiliar impulses appear in groups of people trying things unknown to the society from which they came. When money and success are not the goal, other goals emerge in their place. Nonetheless, most utopian attempts to overcome conflict seem to have resulted only in more serious strife and division. Perhaps this is why Sir Thomas More's word "utopia" means "nowhere." There is nowhere that man can go to strive toward wholeness without recognizing his fragmented nature. Do any utopian experiments take into account both the part of man that wishes to be whole and the part that longs for division? The search for community is generally directed toward someplace "over there." Can the vision of the utopians be pursued here, in the context of life in the world?

The ruins at Mesa Verde, Colorado, represent a communal form of life many hundreds of years old. The cliff-dwellers abandoned their homes in the thirteenth century to relocate in other parts of the Southwest. The Pueblo Indians of today are descended from these ancient people. (Photograph by Paul Kagan)

Notes

CHAPTER 1

[1] John Humphrey Noyes, *History of American Socialisms* (1870; New York: Dover Publications, Inc., 1966), p. 6.

CHAPTER 2

[1] W. P. Swainson, *Thomas Lake Harris and His Occult Teaching* (London: William Rider & Son, Ltd., 1922), p. 8.

[2] Thomas Lake Harris, *The Arcana of Christianity*, Vol. I: *Genesis* (New York: New Church, 1858), p. 383.

[3] *Ibid.*, p. 211.

[4] Thomas Lake Harris, quoted in William Alfred Hinds, *American Communities & Co-operative Colonies* (2nd ed. rev., 1908; New York: Corinth Books, 1961), pp. 425–427.

[5] Thomas Lake Harris, quoted in Herbert W. Schneider and George Lawton, *A Prophet and a Pilgrim* (New York: Columbia University Press, 1942), p. 276.

[6] Thomas Lake Harris, *The Wedding Guest*, Vol. V (Santa Rosa, Calif.: Fountaingrove Press, 1882), p. 134.

[7] Laurence Oliphant, quoted in Schneider and Lawton, p. 264.

[8] Laurence Oliphant, quoted *ibid.*, p. 243.

[9] Thomas Lake Harris, quoted *ibid.*, p. 280.

[10] Alzire Chevaillier, quoted in the San Francisco *Chronicle*, December 13, 1891.

[11] Laurence Oliphant, quoted in Schneider and Lawton, p. 328.

[12] Thomas Lake Harris, *The Arcana of Christianity*, Vol. I, pp. 191–192.

[13] Quoted in Schneider and Lawton, Appendix A, "Experiences of a Sister in the New Life," pp. 509–533.

[14] Thomas Lake Harris, quoted *ibid.*, p. 327.

[15] Laurence Oliphant, quoted *ibid.*, p. 410.

[16] Alzire Chevaillier, quoted in the San Francisco *Chronicle*, December 13, 1891.

[17] Schneider and Lawton, p. xv.

[18] *Ibid.*, p. xiv.

CHAPTER 4

[1] Ray Stannard Baker, "An Extraordinary Experiment in Brotherhood," *The American Magazine*, January, 1907, p. 232.

[2] *Ibid.*, p. 229.

[3] Letter from James Long to Paul Kagan, January 22, 1971.

[4] *Time*, June 21 and July 19, 1968.

[5] Interview with Dr. Judith Tyberg, January 20, 1971.

[6] *The Temple Home Association Explained* (Halcyon, Calif. [ca. 1908]).

[7] "The Founding of Krotona," unpublished typescript in the Krotona archives.

[8] "Ojai: A Cradle of the Future," unpublished typescript in the Krotona archives, ca. 1930.

[9] Interview with Mrs. Albert Powell Warrington.

[10] Alfred Powell Warrington, "Theosophy," *Varieties of American Religion*, ed. Charles S. Braden (Chicago: Willett, Clark & Company, 1936), p. 225.

[11] Annie Besant, "A Lodge of the Theosophical Society," *Theosophical Review*, n.d.

[12] J. Krishnamurti, quoted in Hugh Shearman, *Modern Theosophy* (Adyar, India: The Theosophical Publishing House, 1954), p. 63.

CHAPTER 5

[1] Burnette G. Haskell, "Kaweah, How and Why the Colony Died," *Out West*, September, 1902.

CHAPTER 6

[1] Quoted in the San Francisco *Chronicle*, October 18, 1921.

[2] Agnes Jenkins, quoted *ibid.*

[3] William E. Riker, *A Million Dollar Information Book* (Holy City, Calif.: Holy City Press [ca. 1943]).

[4] *Ibid.*, pp. 6 and 8.

[5] William E. Riker, *The Nun Book* (San Francisco: Enlightener Press [ca. 1915]), p. 21.

[6] William E. Riker, *Devil Worship* (Holy City, Calif.: Holy City Press [ca. 1919]), p. 15.

[7] William E. Riker, quoted in the San Francisco *Chronicle*, April 28, 1929.

[8] William E. Riker, *The Emancipator* (Holy City, Calif.: Holy City Press, 1940).

[9] William E. Riker, quoted in the San Francisco *Chronicle*, July 9, 1935.

[10] William E. Riker, quoted *ibid.*, October 30, 1942.

[11] *Ibid.*, November 4, 1942.

[12] William E. Riker, quoted *ibid.*, December 9, 1942.

[13] Melvin Belli, quoted *ibid.*, December 6, 1942.

[14] William E. Riker, quoted *ibid.*, December 10, 1942.

[15] *Ibid.*, September 4, 1961.

CHAPTER 7

[1] Aldous Huxley, *Tomorrow and Tomorrow and Tomorrow* (New York: Harper & Bros., 1956), p. 84.

[2] Interview with Walter Millsap conducted by Art Wadsworth, May 8, 1964.

[3] Ernest S. Wooster, "They Shared Equally," *Sunset*, July, 1924, p. 23.

[4] Huxley, pp. 87–88.

[5] Ernest S. Wooster, "Bread and Hyacinths," *Sunset*, August, 1924, p. 21.

[6] Quoted in Mellie M. Calvert, "The Llano del Rio Co-operative Colony," unpublished manuscript in the Huntington Library, San Marino, Calif.

[7] Huxley, p. 91.

[8] Job Harriman, "Llano—Community of Ideals," *The Western Comrade*, March, 1917, pp. 8–9.

[9] Job Harriman, Introduction to Ernest S. Wooster, *Communities of the Past and Present* (Newllano, La.: Llano Colonist, 1924), pp. iv and vi.

[10] Wooster, "They Shared Equally," *Sunset*, July, 1924, p. 81.

[11] Wooster, "Bread and Hyacinths," *Sunset*, August, 1924, p. 23.

[12] *Ibid.*, p. 59.

[13] *The Western Comrade*, June, 1916, p. 11.

[14] Huxley, pp. 87 and 89–90.

[15] Wooster, *Communities of the Past and Present*, p. 127.

[16] Gentry Purviance McCorkle, "Wayside Memories of a Tennessee Rebel," unpublished manuscript in the Huntington Library, San Marino, Calif.

[17] Huxley, p. 92.

[18] Robert Carlton Brown, *Can We Co-operate?* (Pleasant Plains, N.Y.: Roving Eye Press, 1940), pp. 132–133.

[19] Ernest S. Wooster, "The Colonists Win Through," *Sunset*, September, 1924, p. 78.

[20] Huxley, pp. 95–96.

[21] Brown, p. 124.

[22] Paul K. Conkin, *Two Paths to Utopia: The Hutterites and the Llano Colony* (Lincoln, Nebr.: University of Nebraska Press, 1965), p. 137.

CHAPTER 8

[1] Finis E. Yoakum, "Finis E. Yoakum's Healing by the Lord," *Pisgah*, July, 1909, pp. 22–23.

[2] Interview with John Bartleman, January 29, 1971.

[3] *Idem.*

[4] *Pisgah Home Songs*. Los Angeles, n.d.

[5] "The Public Services," *Pisgah*, July, 1909.

[6] *Pisgah*, July, 1909, pp. 6, 15, and 21.

[7] Sister Alice M. Kidd, *Ten Years in Pisgah* (Pikeville, Tenn., n.d.).

[8] *Ibid.*

[9] Interview with John Bartleman, January 29, 1971.

[10] James Cheek, *Footprints of a Human Life* (Pikeville, Tenn., n.d.), pp. 106–107.

[11] Interview with H. J. Smith, January 29, 1971.

[12] *Idem.*

CHAPTER 9

[1] From "Zen in America, an Unconditioned Response to a Conditioned World," a promotional leaflet of the California Zen Center, San Francisco.

[2] "The First Practice Period," *Wind Bell*, Fall, 1967, p. 7.

3 "Early History of Tassajara," *ibid.*, pp. 48–49.

4 "Zen in America, an Unconditioned Response to a Conditioned World."

5 "Foods and Meals," *Wind Bell*, Fall, 1967, p. 11.

6 Frances Thompson, "About the Gardens at Tassajara," *Wind Bell*, Summer, 1970, p. 13.

7 Edward Espe Brown, *Wind Bell*, Fall, 1967, p. 12.

8 J. R. Goddard, "Zen Retreat in California: Not for the Frivolous," *The Village Voice*, July 6, 1967.

9 "Tassajara School," *Wind Bell*, Winter, 1970, pp. 26–27.

10 "Guest Season," *Wind Bell*, Fall, 1967, p. 21.

Bibliography

Much of the most important written and pictorial bibliographic material not listed here is located in the Utopian Studies Collection stored at the California Historical Society. This is an archive collected by the author. The collection is an ongoing attempt to acquire and preserve materials from historical and contemporary communes. The archive includes thousands of previously unavailable photographs, pamphlets, documents, publications, and transcribed oral histories of survivors of communal groups. Persons interested in this unique utopian collection may contact the author through the California Historical Society Library, San Francisco.

This bibliography includes works that were read, used, or found interesting in the preparation of the present book. More thorough and exhaustive bibliographies can be found in Robert V. Hine's indispensable work, *California's Utopian Colonies* (San Marino, Calif.: Huntington Library, 1953); Rosabeth Kanter's *Commitment and Community* (Cambridge, Mass.: Harvard University Press, 1972); and Robert S. Fogarty's bibliographical article, "Communal History in America," in *Choice*, Vol. X, No. 4 (June, 1973). Since some of the following books contain material that is relevant to several different chapters, the division of sources by chapter should not be taken as more than a general indication.

CHAPTER 1

Andrews, Edward Deming. *The Gift to Be Simple: Songs, Dances and Rituals of the American Shakers.* New York: J. J. Augustin, 1940. New York: Dover Publications, Inc., 1962.

————. *The People Called Shakers: A Search for the Perfect Society.* New York: Oxford University Press, 1953. New York: Dover Publications, Inc., 1963.

————, and Andrews, Faith. *Shaker Furniture: The Craftsmanship of an American Communal Sect.* New Haven, Conn.: Yale University Press, 1937. New York: Dover Publications, Inc., 1964.

Arndt, Karl J. R. *George Rapp's Harmony Society, 1785–1847.* Rev. ed. Cranbury, N.J.: Fairleigh Dickinson University Press, 1972.

Arnold, Emmy. *Torches Together.* Rifton, N.Y.: Plough Publishing House, 1964.

Bacon, Francis. *New Atlantis* (1629). Oxford, England: Clarendon Press, 1924.

Bailyn, Bernard. *Ideological Origins of the American Revolution.* Cambridge, Mass.: Harvard University Press, 1967.

Bellamy, Edward. *Looking Backward* (1888). Cambridge, Mass.: Harvard University Press, 1967.

Bestor, Arthur Eugene, Jr. *Backwoods Utopias: The Sectarian and Owenite Phases of Communitarian Socialism in America, 1663–1829.* Philadelphia: University of Pennsylvania Press, 1950.

Bridges, Leonard Hal. *American Mysticism*. New York: Harper & Row, 1970.

Buber, Martin. *Paths in Utopias*. Translated by R. F. C. Hull. Boston: Beacon Press, 1960.

Calverton, V. F. *Where Angels Dared to Tread*. Indianapolis, Ind.: Bobbs-Merrill Company, Inc., 1941.

Cohn, Norman. *The Pursuit of the Millennium: Revolutionary Millenarians and Mystical Anarchism of the Middle Ages*. Rev. ed. New York: Oxford University Press, 1970.

Davidson, Marshall B. *Life in America*. 2 vols. Boston: Houghton Mifflin Company, 1951.

Dawson, Christopher. *Religion and the Rise of Western Culture*. New York: Sheed & Ward, Inc., 1950.

Egbert, Donald, and Persons, Stow (eds.). *Socialism in American Life*. 2 vols. Princeton, N.J.: Princeton University Press, 1952.

Gide, Charles. *Communist and Cooperative Colonies*. Translated by Ernest F. Row. London: George G. Harrap, 1930.

Gronlund, Laurence. *The Co-operative Commonwealth* (1884). Cambridge, Mass.: Harvard University Press, 1965.

Hertzler, Joyce Oramel. *The History of Utopian Thought* (1923). New York: Cooper Square Publishers, Inc., 1965.

Hinds, William Alfred. *American Communities & Co-operative Colonies*. 2nd ed. rev., 1908. New York: Corinth Books, 1961.

Holbrook, Stewart H. *Far Corner: A Personal View of the Pacific Northwest*. New York: The Macmillan Company, 1952.

Holloway, Mark. *Heavens on Earth: Utopian Communities in America*. 2nd ed. rev., 1951. New York: Dover Publications, Inc., 1966.

Judah, J. Stillson. *The History and Philosophy of the Metaphysical Movements in America*. Philadelphia: Westminster Press, 1967.

Lockwood, George B. *The New Harmony Movement*. New York: D. Appleton & Co., 1907.

Martin, James J. *Men Against the State: The Exposition of Individualist Anarchism in America, 1827–1908*. DeKalb, Ill.: Adrian Allen Associates, 1953.

More, Thomas. *Utopia* (1516). Baltimore, Md.: Penguin Books Inc, 1967.

Morgan, Arthur. *Edward Bellamy*. New York: Columbia University Press, 1944.

———. *Nowhere Was Somewhere*. Chapel Hill, N.C.: University of North Carolina Press, 1946.

Mumford, Lewis. *The Story of Utopias*. New York: Boni & Liveright, 1922.

Muncy, Raymond Lee. *Sex and Marriage in Utopian Communities: Nineteenth-Century America*. Bloomington, Ind.: Indiana University Press, 1973. Baltimore, Md.: Penguin Books Inc, 1974.

Nordhoff, Charles. *The Communistic Societies of the United States* (1875). New York: Schocken Books, Inc., 1965.

Noyes, John Humphrey. *History of American Socialisms* (1870). New York: Dover Publications, Inc., 1966.

O'Brien, Harriet E. *Lost Utopias*. Perry Walton, 1929.

Parrington, V. *American Dreams: A Study of American Utopias*. 2nd ed. rev. New York: Russell & Russell, 1964.

Plato. *The Republic*. New York: E. P. Dutton & Co., Inc., 1957.

Rhodes, H. V. *Utopia in American Political Thought*. Tucson, Ariz.: University of Arizona Press, 1967.

Robertson, Constance Noyes. *Oneida Community: The Breakup, 1876–1881*. Syracuse, N.Y.: Syracuse University Press, 1972.

——— (ed.). *Oneida Community: An Autobiography, 1851–1876*. With an introduction and prefaces by Constance Noyes Robertson. Syracuse, N.Y.: Syracuse University Press, 1970.

Sanford, Charles L. *The Quest for Paradise*. Urbana, Ill.: University of Illinois Press, 1961.

Shepperson, W. S. *Retreat to Nevada*. Reno, Nev.: University of Nevada Press, 1966.

Swift, Lindsay. *Brook Farm* (1900). New York: Corinth Books, 1961.

Thrupp, Sylvia (ed.). *Millenial Dreams in Action*. The Hague: Mouton, 1962.

Tracy, Joseph. *The Great Awakening*. New York: J. Adams, 1842.

Webber, Everett. *Escape to Utopia*. New York: Hastings House Publishers, Inc., 1959.

Wells, H. G. *A Modern Utopia* (1905). Lincoln, Nebr.: University of Nebraska Press, 1967.

Zablocki, Benjamin. *The Joyful Community*. Baltimore, Md.: Penguin Books Inc, 1971.

CHAPTER 2

Cuthbert, Arthur A. *Life and World-work of Thomas Lake Harris*. Glasgow: 1909.

The Fabulous Treasures of Fountaingrove. San Francisco: Butterfield & Butterfield, 1948. Catalog of Fountaingrove auction.

Harris, Thomas Lake. *The Arcana of Christianity*. Vol. I: *Genesis*. New York: New Church, 1858.

———. *God's Breath in Man and in Humane Society*. Santa Rosa, Calif.: Fountaingrove Press, 1891.

———. *The New Republic*. Santa Rosa, Calif.: Fountaingrove Press, 1891.

———. *The Wedding Guest*. Vol. V. Santa Rosa, Calif.: Fountaingrove Press, 1882.

LeBaron, Gaye. "The Wonder Seeker; Thomas Lake Harris: His Story." Santa Rosa, Calif., 1970. Unpublished manuscript.

Oliphant, Margaret. *Memoir of the Life of Laurence Oliphant and of Alice Oliphant, His Wife*. 2 vols. New York: Harper & Brothers, 1891.

Schneider, Herbert W., and Lawton, George. *A Prophet and a Pilgrim*. New York: Columbia University Press, 1942.

Swainson, W. P. *Thomas Lake Harris and His Occult Teaching*. London: William Rider & Son, Ltd., 1922.

CHAPTER 3

Cabet, Etienne. *Voyage en Icarie*. Paris: 1848.
L'Etoile des Pauvres et des Souffrants. 1881–1883.
L'Etoile du Kansas et de L'Iowa. 1877–1880.
La Jeune Icarie. 1878–1880.
Shaw, Albert. *Icaria: A Chapter in the History of Communism*. New York: 1884.

CHAPTER 4

Part I

Blavatsky, H. P. *Isis Unveiled*. 2 vols. New York: 1877.
———. *The Secret Doctrine*. 3 vols. Point Loma, Calif.: The Aryan Theosophical Press, 1909.
Judge, W. Q. *The Ocean of Theosophy*. Los Angeles: The Theosophy Co., 1937.
Williams, G. M. *Priestess of the Occult: H. P. Blavatsky*. New York: Alfred A. Knopf, Inc., 1946.

Part II

Baker, Ray Stannard. "An Extraordinary Experiment in Brotherhood," *The American Magazine*, January, 1907.
Century Path. 1907–1911.
Greenwalt, Emmett A. *The Point Loma Community in California, 1897–1942: A Theosophical Experiment*. Berkeley, Calif.: University of California Press, 1955.
Harris, Iverson L. *Theosophy Under Fire*. San Diego, Calif.: Point Loma Publications, 1970.
Kagan, Paul, and Ziebarth, Marilyn (ed.). "Eastern Thought on a Western Shore: Point Loma Community," *California Historical Quarterly*, Vol. LII, No. 1 (Spring, 1973).
Long, James A. *Expanding Horizons*. Pasadena, Calif.: Theosophical University Press, 1965.
Lummis, Charles F. "In the Lion's Den," *Out West*, December, 1902.
———. "Those Terrible Mysteries," *Out West*, January, 1903.
New Century. 1897–1903.
New Century Path. 1903–1906.
Raja-Yoga Messenger. 1904–1929.
The Theosophical Path. 1911–1935.

Parts III and IV

Besant, Annie. *Esoteric Christianity; or the Lesser Mysteries*. Hollywood, Calif.: Theosophical Publishing House, 1913.
———. *The Ideals of Theosophy*. Adyar, India: The Theosophical Publishing House, 1912.

———, and Leadbeater, C. W. *Thought Forms*. Wheaton, Ill.: The Theosophical Publishing House, 1901.
Braden, Charles S. (ed.). *Varieties of American Religion*. Chicago: Willett, Clark & Company, 1936.
Comfort, Jane Levington. *From These Beginnings*. New York: E. P. Dutton & Co., Inc., 1937.
Krishnamurti, J. *At the Feet of the Master*. Chicago: The Theosophical Publishing House, n.d.
———. *Commentaries on Living*. Wheaton, Ill.: The Theosophical Publishing House, 1960.
Nethercot, Arthur H. *The First Five Lives of Annie Besant*. Chicago: University of Chicago Press, 1960.
———. *The Last Four Lives of Annie Besant*. Chicago: University of Chicago Press, 1963.
Shearman, Hugh. *Modern Theosophy*. Adyar, India: The Theosophical Publishing House, 1954.
The Temple Artisan. 1903–1973.
The Temple Home Association Explained. Halcyon, Calif., n.d.
Williams, Gertrude Marvin. *The Passionate Pilgrim: A Life of Annie Besant*. New York: Coward-McCann, 1931.

CHAPTER 5

Bancroft Library, Berkeley, Calif. Kaweah Colony Collection.
Commonwealth. 1886–1892.
Haskell, Burnette G. "Kaweah, How and Why the Colony Died," *Out West*, September, 1902.
Hine, Robert V. "A California Utopia: 1885–1890," *Huntington Library Quarterly*, August, 1948.
Lewis, Ruth R. "Kaweah, an Experiment in Co-operative Colonization," *Pacific Historical Review*, November, 1948.
Winser, Phillip. "Memories." San Marino, Calif.: Huntington Library, 1931. Unpublished manuscript.

CHAPTER 6

Riker, William E. *Devil Worship*. Holy City, Calif.: Holy City Press, n.d.
———. *The Emancipator*. Holy City, Calif.: Holy City Press, 1940.
———. *A Million Dollar Information Book*. Holy City, Calif.: Holy City Press, n.d.
———. *The Nun Book*. San Francisco: Enlightener Press, n.d.

CHAPTER 7

Brown, Robert Carlton. *Can We Co-operate?* Pleasant Plains, N.Y.: Roving Eye Press, 1940.
Calvert, Mellie M. "The Llano del Rio Co-operative Colony." San Marino, Calif.: Huntington Library, n.d. Unpublished manuscript.

Conkin, Paul K. *Two Paths to Utopia: The Hutterites and the Llano Colony.* Lincoln, Nebr.: University of Nebraska Press, 1965.

Hoffman, Abraham. "A Look at Llano: Experiment in Economic Socialism," *California Historical Quarterly,* Vol. XL, No. 3 (September, 1961).

Huxley, Aldous. *Tomorrow and Tomorrow and Tomorrow.* New York: Harper & Brothers, 1956.

Kagan, Paul. "Portrait of a California Utopia," *California Historical Quarterly,* Vol. LI, No. 2 (Summer, 1972).

Llano Colonist. 1916–1919 and 1921–1937.

McCorkle, Gentry Purviance. "Wayside Memories of a Tennessee Rebel." San Marino, Calif.: Huntington Library, n.d. Unpublished manuscript.

McDonald, Alexander James. *Llano Co-operative Colony and What It Taught.* Leesville, La.: 1950.

The Western Comrade. 1913–1918.

Wooster, Ernest S. "Bread and Hyacinths," *Sunset,* August, 1924.

———. "The Colonists Win Through," *Sunset,* September, 1924.

———. *Communities of the Past and Present.* Newllano, La.: Llano Colonist, 1924.

———. "They Shared Equally," *Sunset,* July, 1924.

Young, Sid. *The Crisis in Llano Colony, 1935–36.* Los Angeles: 1936.

CHAPTER 8

Cheek, James. *Footprints of a Human Life.* Pikeville, Tenn.: n.d.

Cheek, Mrs. James. *Cherished Memories or the Life of a Tennessee Girl.* Los Angeles: n.d.

Kidd, Sister Alice M. *Ten Years in Pisgah.* Pikeville, Tenn.: n.d.

Lea, Beverly. "Pisgah Grande," *Ventura County Historical Society Quarterly,* Vol. IX, No. 3 (May, 1964).

Los Angeles Public Library. "Dr. F. E. Yoakum" in the California Bibliography File.

Los Angeles *Times.* Clip file and memos.

Pisgah 1909–1921.

Pisgah Home Songs. Los Angeles, n.d.

CHAPTER 9

Brown, Edward Espe. *The Tassajara Bread Book.* Berkeley, Calif.: Shambala Publications, Inc., 1970.

———. *Tassajara Cooking.* Berkeley, Calif.: Shambala Publications, Inc., 1973.

Suzuki, Shunryu. *Zen Mind, Beginner's Mind.* New York: John Weatherhill, Inc., 1970.

Wind Bell. 1961–1973.

CHAPTER 10

Cleland, Robert G. *California in Our Time: 1900–1940.* New York: Alfred A. Knopf, Inc., 1947.

Communities. 1971–1973.

Cushing, Frank Hamilton. *Zuni Breadstuff.* New York: 1920.

De Hartmann, Thomas. *Our Life with Mr. Gurdjieff.* Baltimore, Md.: Penguin Books Inc, 1972.

Fairfield, Richard. *Communes U.S.A.: A Personal Tour.* Baltimore, Md.: Penguin Books Inc, 1972.

Gentry, Curt. *The Last Days of the Late, Great State of California.* New York: G. P. Putnam's Sons, 1968.

Gudde, Erwin Gustav. *California Place Names.* Berkeley, Calif.: University of California Press, 1949.

Hedgepeth, William, and Stock, Dennis. *The Alternative: Communal Life in New America.* New York: The Macmillan Company, 1970.

Hine, Robert V. "Cult and Occult in California," *Pacific Spectator,* Vol. VIII, No. 3 (Summer, 1954).

Hulme, Kathryn. *The Nun's Story.* Boston: Little, Brown and Company, 1956.

———. *Undiscovered Country.* Boston: Atlantic—Little, Brown and Company, 1966.

Huxley, Aldous. *Island.* New York: Harper & Row, Publishers, 1962.

Kagan, Paul. "Perspectives on the Search for Community," *Religion for a New Generation,* ed. Jacob Needleman, A. K. Bierman, and James A. Gould. New York: The Macmillan Company, 1973.

———. "A Portfolio from the Search for Community," *Maitreya I,* ed. Samuel Bercholz and Michael Fagan. Berkeley, Calif.: Shambala Publications, Inc., 1970.

Kaliflower. 1968–1972.

McWilliams, Carey. *Southern California Country.* New York: Duell, Sloan & Pearce, 1946.

Manuel, Frank E. (ed.). *Utopias and Utopian Thought.* Boston: Houghton Mifflin Company, 1966.

Material for Thought. San Francisco: Far West, 1974.

Merton, Thomas. *Mystics and Zen Masters.* New York: Farrar, Straus & Giroux, Inc., 1967.

Needleman, Jacob. *The New Religions.* Rev. ed. New York: Ballantine Books, Inc., 1972.

Sinclair, Upton. *The Autobiography of Upton Sinclair.* New York: Harcourt Brace & World, 1962.

———. *I, Governor of California.* Los Angeles, n.d.

Skinner, B. F. *Walden Two.* New York: The Macmillan Company, 1948.

Reich, Charles. *The Greening of America.* New York: Random House, Inc., 1970.

Roszak, Theodore. *The Making of a Counter Culture.* Garden City, N.Y.: Doubleday & Company, Inc. 1969.